SEMINAR STUDIES IN HISTORY
General Editor: Roger Lockyer

D1322474

Chartism

Second Edition

Edward Royle

Senior Lecturer in History
University of York

LONGMAN
London and New York

LONGMAN GROUP UK LIMITED
*Longman House, Burnt Mill, Harlow, Essex CM20 2JE, UK
and Associated Companies throughout the World.*

Published in the United States of America
by Longman Inc., New York

First published 1980
Second edition 1986

Set in 10/11pt Baskerville (Linotron)
Printed and bound by
Butler and Tanner Ltd Frome and London

ISBN 0 582 35569 9

British Library Cataloguing in Publication Data

Royle, Edward
  Chartism. — 2nd ed — (Seminar
  studies in history)
  1. Chartism
  I. Title   II. Series
  322.4'4'0941   HD8396

  ISBN 0-582-35569-9

Library of Congress Cataloging in Publication Data

Royle, Edward.
  Chartism.

  (Seminar studies in history)
  Bibliography: p.
  Includes index.
  1. Chartism. I. Title. II. Series.
HD8396.R64 1986   332'.2'0941   86-3048
ISBN 0-582-35569-9

Contents

Seminar Studies in History
Founding Editor: Patrick Richardson

Introduction

The Seminar Studies series was conceived by Patrick Richardson, whose experience of teaching history persuaded him of the need for something more substantial than a textbook chapter but less formidable than the specialised full-length academic work. He was also convinced that such studies, although limited in length, should provide an up-to-date and authoritative introduction to the topic under discussion as well as a selection of relevant documents and a comprehensive bibliography.

Patrick Richardson died in 1979, but by that time the Seminar Studies series was firmly established, and it continues to fulfil the role he intended for it. This book, like others in the series, is therefore a living tribute to a gifted and original teacher.

Note on the System of References:
A bold number in round brackets (**5**) in the text refers the reader to the corresponding entry in the Bibliography section at the end of the book. A bold number in square brackets, preceded by 'doc.' [**doc. 6**] refers the reader to the corresponding item in the section of Documents, which follows the main text.

ROGER LOCKYER
General Editor

Acknowledgements

In the preparation of this work I have been greatly assisted by many librarians, especially those at the Manchester Central Library, the British Library, and the Public Record Office. I am also grateful to several generations of students whose insights and errors have alike helped me construct this book, and to countless historians on whose shoulders I sit and whose wisdom is only lamely acknowledged in the bibliography. I have taken the opportunity of a second edition to extend and bring up-to-date the bibliography (preserving so far as possible the existing reference numbers) and incorporate new ideas in the text. The principal changes of emphasis come with discussions of the Newport Rising and the Land Plan. The Conclusion has also been redrafted, though the overall view expressed remains unchanged. My thanks are due to my colleague, Dr James Walvin, who commented on the manuscript and suggested improvements. The errors remain my own.

Abbreviations

Add. Mss	Additional Manuscripts
BPU	Birmingham Political Union
CSU	Complete Suffrage Union
LDA	London Democratic Association
LWMA	London Working Men's Association
NCA	National Charter Association
NUWC	National Union of the Working Classes
PRO	Public Record Office

Part One: The Background

1   The New Society

Britain in the first half of the nineteenth century was the scene of unprecedented economic and social change: so much so that when Friedrich Engels came to describe society in the 1840s he could compare what was happening to the French Revolution of 1789 (**5**). Industrialisation, urbanisation, and the pressure of population growth were transforming the face of the countryside and the lives of the people from decade to decade more surely than any political upheaval. The old certainties were being swept away before the march of material progress.

This was the image. The reality was different in two respects. First, the picture of an industrial revolution sweeping the whole of Britain is a grossly exaggerated one by any modern standards; secondly, many of those men and women who were experiencing this revolution were far from convinced that the new society was an improvement on the old.

The industrial revolution made its greatest impact on those parts of the country having exposed coalfields with readily available supplies of both coal and iron. Here, in South Wales and Central Scotland, in the West Midlands and southern Lancashire, in the West Riding and on Tyneside, a new human geography was being created, with a new technology, new concentrations of industry and population, and new social relationships. With larger units of production and improved communications, regional specialisation was becoming more marked: cotton manufacture in south Lancashire and the Glasgow area; the metal trades in the West Midlands and South Yorkshire; lace and hosiery production in the East Midlands; worsted manufacture around Bradford in the West Riding, at the expense of East Anglia; and woollen production generally in West Yorkshire at the expense of the West Country. Rural industries everywhere were slowly succumbing to the competition of the towns (**13**).

Even so, small units of production were still more common than really large-scale enterprises. The typical textile factory in cotton or worsted production had a hundred or so workers; few had over

1

a thousand; and in the woollen industry the average size of work-force was nearer fifty. The backyard workshops of the Black Country were more typical of the metal trades than large concerns such as those at Dowlais in South Wales or Carron in Scotland. Only a small proportion of the total labour force, even in 1851, worked in factories, and the days of the handloom weaver, though numbered, were still far from over, especially in the woollen trade. The largest manufacturing centre was London, which had scarcely any large-scale industry, though, because small-scale units were no novelty, this important fact was often overlooked by contemporaries eager to comment on what was new. Yet, with a population in 1841 of two million out of a total population in Britain of over eighteen and a half million (with a further eight million in Ireland), London was the greatest economic fact in the life of the nation (**65**).

Manchester, however, was the 'shock city' of the industrial revolution (**20**). Here it was that the images of industrial Britain were formed; here visitors came to peer into the future. This might at first sight seem surprising. In 1851 there were only seven towns in England (and only Glasgow and Edinburgh in Scotland) with populations of over 100,000: Liverpool, Manchester, Birmingham, Leeds, Bristol, Sheffield and Bradford. The total population of these great cities could have been sunk in London, which in the first half of the nineteenth century was expanding by well over 100,000 people each decade. Britain was the most urbanised country in Europe, but it was still a place of medium-to-small towns, overgrown villages and broad acres of open farm land. Even the largest towns were compact. As Geoffrey Best has reminded us, 'At the beginning of Victoria's reign Manchester or Leeds were physically as easy to walk out of as Winchester or Stirling are now' (**18**). But compactness meant overcrowding. The expanding towns compounded the public health nuisances of rural Britain in a way known previously only in London, and too rapid a growth brought with it a burden of badly built, badly drained, unsanitary and unsalubrious dwellings, especially for the lower classes.

What was so shocking about the new industrial towns, epitom-ised by Manchester, was the pace of change, rather than the scale. Within living memory, villages were turning into cities, green fields being swallowed up by grey buildings and smoke. Increasingly the social divisions of the new society were being printed on the new urban map. Town centres were becoming slums squeezed in among commercial developments, as improved communications carried the wealthy to the suburbs and beyond. Town houses were becoming tenements; sunless courts were being built over gardens; railways were marching across living communities like giants, pushing out of their way all that stood in their paths. The modern city was being born (**18**). The division of society into classes, not new in itself, was all the more obvious in the smaller, newer towns. Even Manchester, which was a commercial as well as manufacturing town, had something of a metropolitan air, with an estimated two-thirds of its population in 1836 belonging to the operative classes; but in nearby Stalybridge the proportion was 90 per cent (**105**). In Oldham the economic life of the town, with 11,000 working-class families and 2,000 middle-class families, was dominated by some two hundred households (**17**). It was in towns like these that the economic basis of class consciousness was being laid – a consciousness felt by industrialists and workers alike. All that was needed to turn consciousness into conflict was an economic or political crisis.

This is what happened on occasions between 1790 and 1850, and in the making of Chartism there is a close connection between economic crises and political unrest. William Cobbett once said, 'I defy you to agitate a fellow with a full stomach', and this idea has led Professor W. W. Rostow to devise a 'social tension chart' which attempts to pinpoint those years between 1790 and 1850 when social tension might be expected to be unusually high or low (**14**). His method, based on details of the state of the economy and the price of bread, has suggested for years of high tension, 1795–96, 1801, 1811–13, 1816–17, 1819, 1826–32, 1837–42, 1847–48; and for years of low tension 1790–92, 1798–99, 1802–07, 1809–10, 1815, 1818, 1821–25, 1834–36, 1843–46, 1850. These annual calculations mask seasonal and local variations, but the correlation seems generally good, especially for the Chartist years in the late 1830s and 1840s. The political message of Chartism did find its readiest, most widespread and most violent responses in years of business depression and high bread prices.

The industrial revolution gave the new society both power and problems, and for a generation the latter seemed in danger of paralysing the former. After 1815 recurrent slumps in trade caused chaos on an unprecedented scale. For thirty-five years the birth-pangs of the new society were felt by all classes for, despite a general expansion in the economy, especially in cotton textiles, there were severe periods of cyclical unemployment. The masters were caught in the net of competition. Techniques for producing goods were increasing faster than the markets for those goods. Profit margins in bad years were pared down to nothing, and when no more costs could be saved on machinery attempts were made to economise on labour. Handworkers were kept on to supply extra labour for the booms but were the first to be laid off in the slumps. Long after the wages of the cotton handloom weavers had passed their peak the numbers in the trade continued to grow, right up into the 1830s when there were a quarter of a million of them. Much of the industrial strife of the late 1830s and early 1840s can be traced to depression and attempts to reduce wages. The men fought almost blindly against their hardships, through their trade unions and political societies, but with little success. Some socialist economists argued that higher wages would fortify the home market, but most masters decided that if foreign corn could be imported into Britain, then not only could their men survive on lower wages but also foreigners would be able to use the exchange gained from grain to purchase British industrial goods.

This economic uncertainty is the background to the many controversies of the 1830s and 1840s – whether a ten-hour day in the textile factories was economically possible (it was argued that all the profit was made in the last hour); whether the poor laws were adequate, or whether they simply made the situation worse; whether the Corn Laws should be abolished and whether an aristocratic constitution was appropriate to an industrialising nation; whether the worker was entitled to the full fruits of his own labour, and whether labour as the main contributor to wealth should not also have the vote (**26**). Economic uncertainty was also the background to the feeling which was widely shared in the 1830s that the present system was too frail to last. The new industrial capitalism seemed to contain within itself the seeds of its own destruction; its contradictions were manifest and apparently insoluble. The capacity to produce greater wealth had, it seemed, also produced greater misery; machines were devouring men while competition was driving down wages and profits [**doc. 28**]. Some observers, like Engels and his friend Karl Marx, thought that capitalism was inevitably destroying itself; other socialists, like Robert Owen, daily expected the government to send for them to solve its problems; others, like the Southcottians, prepared to gather in their New Jerusalem at Ashton-under-Lyne to await the Second Coming of Christ (**5, 27**).

The picture of life in early industrial Britain, though, should not be painted in tones of unrelieved gloom. Not all occupational groups suffered by industrialisation; not all urban life was squalid.

Not all rural life matched that picture of blissful contentment which nostalgic town-dwellers sometimes believed it to have been. The towns had much to offer. The historian of Chartism might dwell on the dark side, and select those aspects of working-class life which indicate political concern and social protest, but these need to be set against the broader canvas of what urban life could be. The city had a magnetic quality, and London had long drawn people from all parts of the country. The new towns similarly had many attractions: an intimacy of social intercourse, a diversity of interests, undoubted opportunities, freedom from traditional restraints and hope of economic freedom from parents – all these drew the young and more adventurous to the towns. The social life of the town, whether expressed in the public house and gin palace or in the temperance society and mechanics' institute, had a richness rarely found in the countryside.

It was this vitality which impressed visitors to the new industrial towns of the provinces, and provided their inhabitants with a confidence which expressed itself in the political and economic life of the nation. The early industrial revolution had given to the provinces, and especially to the North of England, the initiative over London in both social and economic progress, and it is this provincialism which makes the history of Britain in the nineteenth century unique. London, of course, remained pre-eminent as the capital city and seat of government, and any movements seeking to be truly national and to influence politicians through public pressure could not afford to neglect London [**doc. 8**], but it was the provinces which provided the dynamism and generated the popular support (**21**).

2 Political Origins

Chartism was a product of the industrial revolution and therefore cannot be understood apart from the economic and social problems of Britain in the 1830s and 1840s, but it was also a political movement with a specific programme for radical reform. So, although economic and social circumstances must play an essential part in the historian's understanding of the incidence of Chartist activity, year by year and area by area, he must also ask *why* the protest movement should have turned to politics.

In the eighteenth century and earlier, the form which crowd activity took was usually determined by the social and economic norms of the community, so that bread riots have to be seen, not as spontaneous outbreaks of irrational though understandable violence, but as attempts of the people to enforce popularly conceived views of the just price. Such notions persisted into the nineteenth century, but increasingly the political response became more marked. The transition involved considerable sophistication for, whereas the link between highly-priced grain and the demand for the just price was immediate and obvious, the link between high food prices or unemployment and an abstract programme for political change was far less clear. Lessons about the nature of the prevailing political and economic system had first to be taught, and something of the structure of power in society understood. In other words, for economic grievances to lead to a political response, the crowd had first to become politically aware.

To say that Chartism was primarily a political movement is to make the claim that the Chartists were politically conscious, but many historians have had grave doubts about how true this was. Most would agree that the leaders of the Chartists were acutely politically aware people, as their writings in their newspapers make clear. We may presume that some who read those articles were also capable of understanding their general import and taking their lessons to heart, but we do not know how far down the ranks this sort of political education could penetrate. Did there come a point, and if so where, at which the political programme became a mere incantation to be recited because it was said to be the solution to all problems, and which was accepted as such, until the promise proved barren with successive failures to achieve any political change? Rather than assume that politics were of primary concern at this level, should one instead be looking for other influences shaping the popular response to hardship, such as deference to paternalism or the desire to reassert the 'moral economy' by direct action, both of which had existed long before the advent of political radicalism and the new industrial society? Finally, one might ask whether the political response in Chartism really was the most appropriate one in circumstances of economic hardship?

The origins of the radical political programme adopted by the Chartists can be traced back to the third quarter of the eighteenth century, though in a more general way the nineteenth-century radicals also saw themselves as part of the Leveller tradition of the seventeenth. In 1774–75 James Burgh, a disciple of the radical Dissenter, Richard Price, published his *Political Disquisitions*, in which he renewed the call for manhood suffrage, and in 1776 John Wilkes echoed the cry in a speech in Parliament. From this time onwards the extension of the franchise was firmly established, alongside shorter parliaments, as an essential plank in the reformers' platform.

This same year, 1776, saw the outbreak of the American rebellion and the publication of Major John Cartwright's pamphlet, *Take Your Choice*, which set out the essence of what was to become the Chartist programme, with universal suffrage, annual parliaments and vote by ballot. Unlike Burgh, however, who was willing to contemplate the replacement of Parliament with an alternative assembly (which is what the Americans did), Cartwright more moderately hoped that the Commons could be brought to reform itself. Both Burgh's and Cartwright's views were to co-exist within British radicalism, the latter generally predominating.

Great though Cartwright's contribution was, however, by far the most important of all the eighteenth-century reformers was Thomas Paine, who had cut his radical teeth in the American revolution with his pamphlet *Common Sense* and his *Crisis* papers. Back in England in the early 1790s, he went on to celebrate the French Revolution with a vigorous defence of its principles, and an equally vigorous attack on the British system in his two-part *Rights of Man* (1791–92). These products of Paine's fluent pen were to become the foundation documents of nineteenth-century British radicalism. As journeymen and apprentices in London, Sheffield,

Norwich, Manchester and other towns and villages up and down the country read or heard read aloud extracts from the *Rights of Man* and similar political pamphlets which rapidly became popular, the theme of the necessity for radical political reform began to strike home. The government clamped down on such seditious works, and Paine left for France, his parting shot being his most radical work, *A Letter addressed to the Addressers on the late Proclamation* in which he called for a National Convention elected on adult male suffrage. Though this letter was never as widely circulated as *Rights of Man*, the idea and the examples of America and France were to remain with the radicals and shape the Chartist reaction in 1839.

Paine was both a political pamphleteer and an able political theorist, advocating political, economic and social reforms which only the twentieth century has taken seriously enough to embody in legislative programmes. Even his warmest disciples do not seem to have fully absorbed his teachings on social welfare (including old-age pensions), currency reform, and the foundation of political rights in abstract reasoning. Historical appeals to lost Saxon liberties, denunciations of the Norman Conquest (and sometimes the dissolution of the monasteries as well) long continued to be heard, and for many the Bible continued (in the Puritan tradition) to be regarded as a republican's handbook, even though Paine thought the very reverse. Paine was popular and influential, but his ideas were absorbed rather than fully understood.

The late eighteenth century also bequeathed to the nineteenth the beginnings of radical organisation, as provincial constitutional societies and the London Corresponding Society (founded 1792) met to discuss, educate their members, and prepare for the day when England and Scotland would throw off their monarchical and aristocratic chains and walk in the full freedom of democracy. How far this brand of radicalism had petered out by the end of the 1790s, or how far it had been suppressed but survived as an underground tradition, is a matter hotly disputed among historians (**22**). Certainly, formal political organisations largely disappeared, but in some parts of the country a minority of extremists does seem to have maintained a revolutionary tradition of subversive activity; and, more respectably, Major Cartwright continued his patient propagandism while Francis Place, master tailor and former member of the London Corresponding Society, began his equally patient career as wire-puller extraordinary in the no-man's-land between the popular and respectable worlds of London radicalism.

The events of the 1790s, when the lower-class wing of the British reform movement took heart from the French Revolution, proved to be a turning point in the development of radicalism. Although the reformers were a small minority of the population, the skilled and literate artisans had now, if not before, taken the step into political consciousness and had accepted the programme of radical political reform. Thereafter, the campaign for reform was to rouse considerable feeling in the ranks below those of the tradition-al political classes, as this awareness spread to those inhabitants of the new society who were about to be called 'the working classes'.

The 1790s had seen an explosion in the output of printed mate-rial of all kinds, and the man who above all continued this process in the early nineteenth century was William Cobbett (1763–1835), a Tory yeoman who belonged to old England by birth and convic-tion, but who in 1804 read Paine's *Decline and Fall of the English System of Finance* and was converted by it to currency reform and radicalism. In 1816 he decided to address his *Weekly Political Register* to a wider audience, dropped the price from 1s 0½d (5p) to 2d (1p), and had a quite remarkable success as his paper found its way into homes throughout the country. In rural Yorkshire at Malton, radical James Watson's mother was in the habit of reading it and, as Samuel Bamford, a handloom weaver from Middleton near Manchester, recalled: Cobbett's works 'were read on nearly every cottage hearth in the manufacturing districts of South Lancashire, in those of Leicester, Derby, and Nottingham; also in many of the Scottish manufacturing towns.' The message was loud and clear, and readily understood. 'He directed his readers to the true cause of their sufferings – misgovernment; and to its proper corrective – parliamentary reform' (**47a, 41**).

In this sort of way, during the years of distress which followed the French wars, parliamentary reform became the cry. Local Hampden Clubs were founded following the example set by Major Cartwright; groups of Political Protestants gathered to discuss events of the day at the time of the 1818 general election; and Henry 'Orator' Hunt raised crowds to heights of enthusiasm. Other radical publishers followed Cobbett in issuing cheap papers for the people, one of the most influential being Jonathan Wooler, whose *Black Dwarf* brought a young unemployed tinsmith named Richard Carlile into the ranks of the radicals. Carlile then turned publisher himself and made his life's work the reissuing of the works of Thomas Paine (**32**).

By organisation, by publication and by oratory, the emergent radical leadership drove home the message to their working-class audiences that the rights of man belonged to them as well as to the rich, and that their sufferings would be permanently relieved only when they achieved full political rights. But if the writings and recollections of contemporaries are to be believed, the advancement of political consciousness was also promoted by certain key events in working-class experience. The American and French revolutions had helped to shape the older generation; the new generation of the early nineteenth century was to be baptised at St Peter's Fields, Manchester, on 16 August 1819 – the occasion of the 'Peterloo' massacre – when eleven people were killed and hundreds injured as the local yeomanry cavalry charged the unarmed crowd of reformers who had come to Manchester from all the industrial villages and towns in the area, carrying banners and dressed in festive clothing, to hear 'Orator' Hunt. They were dispersed in panic, carrying back to their communities their witness of the brutal assault (**41**). The event sank deep into the folk memory of Lancashire villages and further afield. Richard Carlile, who was present on the platform with Hunt, took back to London the story of the 'Manchester massacre', and working folk everywhere were given the opportunity to read about and to identify themselves with those who had actually been there.

If this was the baptism, then a dozen years later came the confirmation, with the agitation for the Reform Bill. This time the initiative lay with the Whig politicians, and the leadership came from the middle-class reformers. With the collapse of the Duke of Wellington's Tory government in 1830 and the advent to power of Whig ministers in favour of reform, a vast public opinion was generated across the country by a strange assortment of groups, from country gentlemen disgruntled by Catholic emancipation to pushing industrialists who hoped to enter the world of political power and shape it for themselves (**21, 24**). But the reformers' position was hardly secure and the middle class itself was not that dominant force which it tried to appear to be. The limited extent of industrialisation by 1830 meant that the manufacturing sector was still of minor importance when compared with land, and the position of the middle classes in society was neither large nor particularly stable. Like the working classes they were still much fragmented, hardly a class at all, and their economic position was always vulnerable. In these circumstances both Whig politicians and middle-class reformers were happy to have the support of working-class crowds whose presence lent an appearance of reality to blustering threats of revolution. And threats there were: there is little to choose between the later violent language of the Chartists, which was to earn them time in gaol, and the revolutionary talk of respectable middle-class citizens agitating for their Reform Bill in 1832. Edward Baines, junior, son of the editor of the *Leeds Mercury* and a leader of the industrial bourgeoisie of Leeds, was to live to regret his words in 1832, when the Chartists threw them back in his teeth less than a decade later.

The trick appeared to work, the working classes never really established for themselves an independent reform agitation, and a moderate Bill was passed to reform the worst abuses of the system, establishing a uniform £10 householder franchise in parliamentary boroughs and giving separate representation to some of the larger industrial towns. But the anomalies of the unreformed system had in some cases meant a relatively open franchise, as in Preston which had elected Henry Hunt in 1830. The Tory, Richard Oastler, grimly noted that the effect of the 1832 Act was to enfranchise money: it was for him a truly bourgeois revolution (**51**).

Those still excluded, however, also gained something valuable from the events of 1830–32 – that is, experience. The sense of betrayal fortified the popular radical leaders and strengthened their positions, for the respectable reformers had proved good teachers. For over two years they had been urging the overwhelming import-ance of political reform, and they had shown how, by the external pressure of noise and threats, it could be achieved. The clamour of the 'May Days' of 1832 was widely believed to have secured the Reform Act, and the lesson was well learned.

Furthermore, the years between the beginning of the crisis (1830) and the first drafting of the points of the Charter (1837) saw no fewer than five general elections, three of them under the new franchise, and, although not all seats were contested every time, more than usual were. Some places also had by-elections, and Huddersfield had two. Elections were traditionally the times at which non-electors could participate in politics, but not since the reign of Queen Anne had there been anything quite like this. Newspaper reports, especially of contests in the industrial towns, show eager participation by crowds of people with clear views of their own. The political system was itself thereby promoting the politicisation of the emergent working class.

In this process, leadership was essential: this was still largely supplied by London. From the capital, reformers in the country were appealed to, cajoled, reinforced, and organised through the agency of the radical press. Cobbett had blazed the trail (and was to continue active until his death in 1835); Richard Carlile had spent longer inside gaol than outside for publishing the blasphemous views of Paine; but the hero of the 1830s was undoubtedly Henry Hetherington, leading publisher of the unstamped press (**50, 28, 29**).

The world of London journeymen and their trade societies in the 1820s had proved fertile ground, not only for the development of political ideas, but also for socialist theories of co-operative production and distribution. From among these co-operative ventures in London in the late 1820s emerged a group of working men who provided the first coherent working-class radical leadership. Hetherington (1792–1849) was a printer, born in London, who in 1821 had become involved with the first Owenites. In 1824 he had been one of the working men associated with the foundation of the London Mechanics' Institute, where Thomas Hodgskin had lectured on the labour theory of value. Closely associated with Hetherington were James Watson (1799–1874) who had first come to London to help in Carlile's campaign, and William Lovett (1800–77) who had come from his native Cornwall to London to seek work as a cabinet maker (**47a, 42**). Both Lovett and Watson had also joined the Owenites, and with Hetherington were leading members of the British Association for the Promotion of Co-operative Knowledge, and its offspring, the Metropolitan Trades Union. Out of the latter, at the height of the Reform Bill crisis in 1831, they produced the National Union of the Working Classes to spearhead the working-class campaign for a real reform bill.

In 1819 the government had tightened up the newspaper stamp law in order to suppress papers like Cobbett's *Weekly Political Register*, Wooler's *Black Dwarf* and Carlile's *Republican* by defining cheap weekly papers as newspapers whether or not they actually contained news. The effect had been to force up the price of such papers to 6d ($2\frac{1}{2}$p), which severely restricted their circulation among the working classes (**23**). In 1830 several publishers, led by John Doherty in Manchester and William Carpenter in London, challenged this law openly by publishing cheap unstamped papers. Other publishers rapidly followed suit, notably Hetherington, assisted by his friends Lovett and Watson.

Hetherington's most famous paper was the *Poor Man's Guardian*, issued from 31 July 1831 as a periodical in defiance of the law.

Shortly afterwards he was joined by a young Irish lawyer, James O'Brien (he adopted the middle name of Bronterre, by which he is best known), who, as editor of the *Poor Man's Guardian*, rapidly established himself as the foremost theorist of working-class radicalism. Through the *Guardian* he preached class consciousness and the political and economic rights of the working classes, and sought to place the class struggle within its European context. At its height the *Poor Man's Guardian* sold 16,000 copies a week, and was read by a great many more people, though one can never be sure how many of those readers actually understood the message in its entirety.

Led by the *Poor Man's Guardian*, the unstamped press flourished in London and the provinces, feeding working-class radicalism with a new and independent sense of purpose. More than this, it fostered organisation. Networks of booksellers and newsagents, publishers and street-vendors, were built up. Commitment to the cause was demonstrated not only by buying an unstamped paper but also by contributing pennies to support those 'victims' who were imprisoned for selling the unstamped, or by volunteering to join the ranks of the victims. Hundreds of young men, as well as some women, were caught up in a veritable army to fight the war. By 1834 an important battle had been won when the *Poor Man's Guardian* was declared by a London jury to be a legal publication after all, but, as the economic position of the country improved in the mid-1830s, the impetus was lost. In 1835 the stamp was reduced to 1d (½p), enabling the respectable press to compete with the unstamped, while still effectively pricing the idea of a truly working-class newspaper out of the market. The extraordinary thing about the Chartists is that they did manage to support one such paper, the *Northern Star*, against all the odds (**28, 29**).

The consequences of the war of the unstamped are difficult to over-estimate. A generation of radical leaders cut its teeth on the struggle. Some, like George Julian Harney, who helped Hetherington in his shop and was three times imprisoned, soon emerged as national figures (**53**); others, like the printer and journalist, Joshua Hobson of Huddersfield, were important in the provinces (**60**). The rapid spread of Chartism in the late 1830s cannot be understood unless the impact of the unstamped is fully appreciated. From Hetherington, Lovett, Watson and O'Brien at the top, through to the lowest unemployed street-vendor at the bottom, working-class radicals had established a network of organisation and chain of command which could be revived when the occasion demanded it.

The war of the unstamped had been declared in London, though it had been fought across the country. The early 1830s saw two further campaigns which were distinctly provincial in origin. Whereas much London activity can be traced back to the political tradition founded in the late eighteenth century, the provinces (especially the textile areas of Lancashire and Yorkshire) were responding more directly to the problems of the new society, first by agitating for a reduction of working hours in the factories, and then by fighting against the imposition of the Poor Law Amendment Act.

Neither of these causes was purely working-class in nature, for support and even leadership came also from individuals of the traditional ruling classes. Paternalism could join with a working-class sense of natural justice in opposition to the pushing new factory masters, self-satisfied political economists and centralising bureaucrats, who mistook for signs of progress those changes which were subverting the old order of creation [**doc. 16**].

The leadership of the factory movement illustrates the complexity of the situation. The initial moves for legislation regulating hours of work for women and children in the new cotton factories had come from the elder Sir Robert Peel (father of the Conservative leader) and Robert Owen, both of them Tories and both of them pioneer capitalists in the cotton industry; the Ten Hours movement in Yorkshire in the 1830s was inspired by a Tory land steward, Richard Oastler, and led in Parliament by his friend Michael Sadler, until the latter lost his seat as a consequence of the Reform Act. Then Lord Ashley, another Tory, took up the cause, but without the backing of the younger Peel and the Conservative leadership in Parliament. Meanwhile in Lancashire a movement towards even shorter working hours was being directed by the Owenite trade union leader, John Doherty, and the radical factory master from Todmorden, John Fielden, with additional fire and fury supplied by the Tory Wesleyan preacher, Joseph Rayner Stephens (**30, 48, 51, 61a**).

Unlike the parliamentary reform movement, in which the respectable leadership had its own aims, which divided the campaign into two mutually suspicious halves, these leaders of the factory movement were united with the working men in their fight against the inhumanities of factory labour. Most of them had little to gain personally from their involvement, the origins of which

14

were moral and religious rather than narrowly economic and self-seeking. This gave the factory movement the quality of a moral campaign, closely related to the successful struggle against slavery on which so many nineteenth-century pressure groups were modelled. Whereas the political reform movement of the London artisans was based on a sense of outraged natural rights, demanding an abstract programme of reform, the campaign in the North was to assume more the nature of a crusade. The former represented the head of the movement; the latter was the heart, and without it Chartism would have been just another episode in the struggle of the artisans for political reform. With it, a new element entered which was to make Chartism a transforming political and social experience.

In the popular journals and radical speeches of the 1830s the image was built up of the Great Whig Betrayal – one of the myths on which, along with 'Peterloo', working-class conciousness was founded. The limited nature of the Reform Act itself was one element in this betrayal, but practically everything the Whigs did between 1830 and 1841, from suppression of the 'Swing' incendiary riots in the countryside of 1830 to the threat to civil liberties implied by the coercion of the Irish in 1833 and the treatment of the Canadian rebels of 1837, was built up as evidence of a great conspiracy by the pseudo-liberal Whigs against the people (**38a**). No item of Whig legislation contributed more to this feeling than the Poor Law Amendment Act of 1834.

This Act, which proposed to abolish outdoor relief for the able-bodied poor, who were to be forced to find work or face the unpleasant alternative of the workhouse, aroused hostility from the start. The old Poor Law could in theory be as unpleasant as the new, but locally it had often been humanely administered with much outdoor relief going to the genuine unemployed. The Royal Commission on the Poor Laws thought this wasteful, degrading, and a reason for the apparently increasing problem of poverty; hence the new Act. In fact we now know that in many areas the Act made scarely any difference, but what greeted the proposals was based on fear and suspicion: this latest product of the political economists was instinctively felt to be a threat to the traditional rights, and indeed lives, of the poor.

The implementation of the Act was begun in 1835, a year of good harvests and general prosperity in the South of England, where the burden of the poor rates and the low level of wages were real problems. Here the Act could have some relevance, and there was only sporadic opposition. But the experience of the industrial areas was quite different. Here periods of boom, with long working hours, alternated with periods of slump and widespread unemployment. The workhouse test was largely irrelevant. Worse still, the assistant poor law commissioners moved into the North in 1837 as the country was entering into one of the worst and most prolonged periods of depression in the nineteenth century (**31**).

The implementation of the Act met with resistance from the same forces which were campaigning for a Factory Act: localism, Toryism, and working-class radicalism, against the new political economy and heartless bureaucracy as symbolised by Edwin Chadwick, who in 1833 had taken time off from the Royal Commission on the Poor Laws to serve on a Royal Commission on the Employment of Children in Factories which had produced a report as favourable to the masters as was reasonably possible. The outrage of the North spilled over into violence as attempts were made to prevent the new poor law unions from electing their boards of guardians, and then, defeated in this, to prevent the boards from electing their secretaries and getting to work. Led by Lawrence Pitkethly, Oastler's right-hand man, the Huddersfield crowds used controlled violence to delay the implementation of the Act for over a year, while in Fielden's Todmorden the existing workhouses were closed and no new ones built. The anti-poor law movement passed over into Chartism during 1838 and 1839, taking with it a legacy of organisation, leadership, experience, and hatred (**31a**).

The most important fact of all, though, about the legacy of the 1830s to Chartism, was the sense of unity of purpose which had been built up. Members of political unions, vendors of the unstamped, trades unionists, members of Short Time Committees (for an eight- or ten-hour day), and opponents of the poor law were not different people. Local studies show that the same people were involved in all these activities and were thinking of them as part of a whole. Furthermore, they were thinking not just in local terms, but were conscious of events in other parts of the country. London radicals might have different emphases from the men of the North or of Scotland; the West Country might have different problems from those of the North East; but horizons seem to have been widening, thanks partly to lecture tours from a leadership usually based on London, and partly to the radical press. Though it may be convenient for the historian to speak of the London artisan tradition or the economic problems of the factory districts, the North too had its artisans and politicians, and the South had its economic problems. Regional diversity persisted, but within a national framework. By the late 1830s it is possible to argue that a radical working-class presence existed in all the industrial areas of Britain, and on this presence was founded the campaign for the People's Charter (**22, 23a**).

Part Two: Development

3 1836–1840: The Years of Promise Unfulfilled

The idea of a people's 'Charter' was rooted in the myth of Magna Carta which was held to have been a statement of popular rights against the arbitrary authority of the king. Indeed the supposed right to bear arms given in Magna Carta was to be given by the Chartists as a legal justification for the arming and drilling which they were to practise 'in their own self-defence' [**doc. 6**]. The 1832 Reform Act had also been presented in this light as a 'new' Magna Carta, and its failure to be such prompted working-class radicals to demand a true Charter of their own. In 1831, at the height of the Reform Bill crisis, the radical publisher William Strange had produced a pamphlet costing 3d (1¼p) entitled *The New Charter, humbly addressed to the King and both Houses of Parliament; proposed as the basis of a Constitution for the Government of Great Britain and Ireland, and as a substitute for the Reform Bill rejected by the Lords.* Three years later, when the fears of the *Poor Man's Guardian* about the nature of middle-class reform had been fully justified, the paper carried a characteristically pungent editorial, headed 'Order! Liberty!! and the Charter!!!'

Despite the strong language of class consciousness, however, which marks the popular radical literature of the early 1830s, there was in fact no complete severance of relations between radicals of the middle and working classes. The National Union of the Working Classes, unlike the *Poor Man's Guardian*, had given tentative support to the Reform Bill (though not to the final Act). It was not a wholly representative body, and its leaders felt able in the mid-1830s to co-operate with erstwhile rivals in Place's National Political Union to attack the newspaper stamp. Respectable educationalists, like Henry Brougham, Charles Knight of the Society for the Diffusion of Useful Knowledge and Dr J. R. Black, had joined with Francis Place and John Arthur Roebuck, Radical MP for Bath, to establish in 1835 a Society for the Promotion of the Repeal of the Stamp Duties, and Roebuck had even gone so far as to copy the methods of Carpenter and Hetherington in defiance of the law (**29**). By 1836 men like Place and Roebuck had

18

become no less aware than men like Hetherington and Lovett that the Reform Act had been a sham. Radicals who had believed in the Bill in 1831–32 could now see that it had strengthened existing structures and that radicalism had been defeated (**25**). The time was ripe for the various classes to come together again in a campaign for further political reform in the tradition stretching back to Major Cartwright and the late eighteenth century. Radicals who had struggled against the newspaper stamp were to carry their co-operative efforts into early Chartism. When the same men emerged defeated from Chartism in 1849, they were to resume the campaign (this time successfully) for the abolition of all the hated 'taxes on knowledge' (**32**).

The campaign of 1835–36 was co-ordinated by the Society for the Promotion of the Repeal of the Stamp Duties, the working-class members of which were formed into an Association of Working Men to procure a Cheap and Honest Press; this in turn, in June 1836, became 'The London Working Men's Association for benefiting – politically, socially and morally – the useful classes'. Place and Black acted as midwives to this latter body, of which Lovett was secretary and Hetherington treasurer. The Association itself was intended exclusively for London working men, but honorary members were permitted from the provinces and from the higher classes, and these included Place, Black, Augustus Beaumont, MP, Colonel Perronet Thompson, MP, Bronterre O'Brien, and William Carpenter, with John Fielden, Roebuck, Oastler and Feargus O'Connor being amongst those subsequently added. Enquiries were soon received from other parts of London and the provinces, but the Corresponding Societies Act (1799) prevented the LWMA from setting up branch associations, so when local associations were formed they were actually independent of the parent body, though they were often the creation of its propaganda and its missionaries (**1**).

Assiduously the LWMA members met and discussed; their object was political education and, through education, pressure for change. An address was issued to the Belgian working classes (1836), enquiries were instituted as to the condition of the working classes in various London trades, but, above all, the issue of universal suffrage was discussed. By October 1836, the Association had already adopted resolutions containing five of the six points of the Charter, and all six points were embodied in a petition prepared for submission to the House of Commons in January 1837. Public meetings were held, associations in the provinces were urged to co-operate, and on 31 May 1837 a meeting was arranged at the British Coffee House, Cockspur Street, Charing Cross, between members of the LWMA and Radical Members of Parliament, to consider the petition, which had already been signed by some 3,000 people. Out of this meeting, adjourned to 7 June, came a joint committee of six MPs (Daniel O'Connell, J. A. Roebuck, J. T. Leader, Charles Hindley, W. Sharman Crawford, and Colonel Thompson) and six working men (Hetherington, John Cleave, Watson, Richard Moore, Lovett and Henry Vincent) which issued its famous statement of the Six Points and set about to prepare draft legislation on the subject. Then there were many delays, Roebuck, Thompson and Crawford lost their seats at the 1837 general election, and O'Connell lost the confidence of working men, with his attacks on trade unions and support of the new poor law. Finally, it appears that Lovett, aided by Place, actually drew up the draft Bill which, with minor amendments, was published in May 1838 as the People's Charter (**88**).

Chartism was therefore born out of the tradition of articulate, politically conscious artisan radicalism in London, with the encouragement of radicals among the higher classes. Though conscious of class, it was not a document conceived in hatred and conflict: it was a document appropriate to the social structure of the London trades which, in the prosperous years of the mid-1830s, did not easily divide into mutually antagonistic classes. The same could be said of Birmingham, where parallel developments were occurring.

The Birmingham Political Union had taken the lead in the agitation of 1830–32 and had successfully united middle- and working-class radicals in a common cause. But Thomas Attwood, the radical banker and now MP for Birmingham, whose creation the Birmingham Political Union was, had suffered the same disappointment over the Reform Act as the other radicals. He had looked to a reformed parliament to abandon the gold base of the currency (which amounted to a credit squeeze) in order to prosper small businesses such as were characteristic of Birmingham. Obedient to Cobbett's maxim, however, he had not tried further agitation while stomachs were full in the mid-1830s, but in May 1837, as depression set in once more, he revived the BPU to agitate for a further measure of parliamentary reform. At first the Union's programme, promulgated at a mass meeting on Newhall Hill on 19 June 1837, demanded only triennial parliaments and household suffrage and did not mention the equalisation of electoral districts, but in November it came out fully for universal suffrage. As the economic depression deepened yet further, and as the government did nothing about it, the BPU became more extreme in its demands and more active. Like the LWMA it adopted the idea of sending missionaries to encourage reform movements in other parts of the country, and John Collins was sent to Glasgow in March 1838 to liaise with radicals there. On 14 May the BPU adopted a national petition for reform, and the following week a delegation attended a Glasgow reform meeting at which 200,000 people were said to be present. The LWMA representatives were also present, and for the first time the ideas of a National Petition and a People's Charter were presented on the same platform [**doc. 1**]. The BPU men now accepted the full Six Points of Manhood Suffrage, Annual Parliaments, the Ballot, Payment of MPs, Equal Electoral Districts, and the Abolition of the Property Qualifications for Parliament, and the LWMA accepted the idea of a national petition as a means of bringing the whole Charter to the attention of Parliament. The beginning of Chartism in England can therefore be dated from the great rally held in Birmingham on 6 August 1838, at which these arrangements were formally adopted, but already the campaign had become a national one (**71a**).

Although it is right to emphasise the origins of Chartism in London and Birmingham, to concentrate exclusively on the LWMA and the BPU is to rob other organisations of their share in the groundswell of activity, which in some cases can be dated back to 1835 when a number of Radical Associations were founded in Scotland and the North of England. In September 1835 Feargus O'Connor, who had just lost his Irish seat in Parliament and was moving in on the English radical scene, founded the Marylebone Radical Association, which was active in the campaign against the newspaper stamp. In December 1835 he went on a tour of the North founding similar bodies, so that when he returned there in the autumn of the following year he was already established as an English leader, able to take his place alongside J. R. Stephens and Richard Oastler (**54**). This activity was quite apart from that of the LWMA, whose association with O'Connell was anathema to O'Connor (**54a**).

Hetherington's protégé, George Julian Harney, and his former editor, Bronterre O'Brien, were also alienated from the LWMA by its middle-class links, especially with O'Connell, and in 1837 in London a rival party began to form around Harney, O'Brien and O'Connor. In January, with the help of veteran Spenceans Allen

Davenport and the radical tailor Charles Neesom, Harney began
the East London Democratic Association, to appeal to the more
depressed trades of London, such as the weavers of Spitalfields,
and to promote their moral and political position 'by dissemi-
nating the principles propagated by that great philosopher and
redeemer of mankind, the Immortal Thomas Paine'. At first
Harney hoped his association would be able to establish a friendly
alliance with the LWMA, but by the spring of 1838 there was a
clear breach between the two (**53**).

O'Brien had parted company with the LWMA somewhat earlier
over its attitude to the formation of the Central National Association, the origins of which can be traced to August 1836, when
J. B. Bernard of the Cambridgeshire Tenant Farmers' Association
(a currency reformer of the Attwood school) approached the
LWMA with a view to establishing a common cause. The move
was supported by Bell's *London Mercury*, of which O'Brien was co-
editor, but opposed by Hetherington's *London Dispatch*. O'Connor
gave his support to Bernard, and the Central National Association
resulted in March 1837. It is significant mainly as a reminder of
O'Connor's abiding interest in the land and its problems, for it
never really came to anything, despite its grand title. O'Brien
disliked the particular currency theories advanced by Bernard,
and left the *Mercury* (which shortly afterwards merged with the
Dispatch), and O'Connor switched his attentions to the North,
where in November he started the *Northern Star*. Meanwhile,
Harney's East London Democratic Association had fallen on hard
times, and in May 1838 was reorganised as the London Democratic Association in direct opposition to the LWMA (**54a, 63b**).

By the time of the Birmingham meeting of August 1838, therefore, a great deal of progress had been made on several fronts,
particularly by O'Connor in the West Riding and to a lesser extent
by Harney in London. But the rivalry of the leaders should not be
mistaken for division in the localities. Though a local radical group
might well have looked in preference to O'Connor or Hetherington,
Harney or Lovett, the two were not mutually exclusive. Chartism
was becoming a unified national movement, in spite of its leaders.

O'Connor had not been the only organiser on tour. During the
summer of 1837 the LWMA sent Hetherington, Vincent and
Cleave on lecture tours, and all three were active in Yorkshire
promoting Working Men's Associations. As R. G. Gammage, first
historian of Chartism, later recalled, Hetherington was no great
orator but he had a tremendous reputation as leader of the war

of the unstamped. This had made his name a household word: 'it was not his mission to create new elements but to cement those already in existence, and these elements he found in every town he visited' (**7**).

During the summer of 1838 the pace quickened. Between the Glasgow meeting in May and the Birmingham one in August, the Great Northern Union held its first meeting in Leeds to rally the North, while Vincent, Hetherington, Cleave, Watson, Moore and Hartwell of the LWMA were in constant demand as lecturers. On 17 September a public meeting was held in the Palace Yard, Westminster, chaired by the high Bailiff and addressed by Roebuck, O'Brien and the LWMA speakers listed above, as well as by a number of provincial delegates, including Robert Lowery from Newcastle, and Feargus O'Connor. Chartism had already outgrown its origins. The whole country was now astir. In November 1837 Hetherington had founded Working Men's Associations in Welshpool, Newtown and Llanidloes; in May 1838 Vincent had had a rapturous welcome in the West Country at Bath; but the most spectacular progress was being made in the North, already alive with the short time and anti-poor law agitations. During the summer of 1838 the three movements became as one. Central to this development was the *Northern Star*, first published in Leeds by Joshua Hobson in November 1837, through which O'Connor was able to complete the takeover of the earlier agitations by Chartism, and to make himself the successor to Stephens and Oastler as the great popular leader of the textile districts (**54a**).

During 1837, the anti-poor law campaign had emerged as a great popular movement which reached a climax at a rally held on Hartshead Moor (Peep Green) between Huddersfield, Bradford and Leeds in May, attended by many of the most popular figures of the time, from Oastler, Owen and Stephens, to O'Connor, O'Brien and Hetherington and an audience of between 100,000 and 250,000 people. In the months thereafter, local anti-poor law struggles, political societies, and revived Owenism (in the form of branches of the Association of All Classes of All Nations) spread side by side, preparing the way for the great surge of political activity in 1838. The first major outdoor meeting in the North organised explicitly for Chartism, on Kersal Moor, near Manchester, on 24 September 1838, saw the same sorts of crowds and the same passions as at the Hartshead Moor meeting the previous year. Only the emphasis was different, for by now the anti-poor law campaign was in retreat and the people were being persuaded that what direct action had failed to achieve, a parliament elected by universal suffrage would soon put right. The tone of the meeting was set by J. R. Stephens, who proclaimed to the crowd the economic basis of his support for Chartism – it was, he said, 'a knife and fork question' [**doc. 2**]. This was a far cry from the political debates of the London artisans.

The ostensible purpose of the Kersal Moor meeting was to enable the people to elect their delegates to a National Convention, to be held in London early the following year, and the work of the winter was directed largely to this end, with further mass meetings and lecture tours. The idea of a Convention was not, initially, to set up a parallel assembly to Parliament (though this was doubtless in the minds of some delegates), but to organise the National Petition and to see it through Parliament. The aim of the Chartists was to throw all their efforts into collecting signatures for the petition: basing themselves on the BPU they looked for the same success as the middle classes had enjoyed in 1832. As the lecturers toured the country, stirring up support for the petition and themselves during the winter of 1838–39, they saw evidence of the grim determination of their followers to exert the maximum of pressure for reform. In Newcastle upon Tyne in December, Harney found the Winlaton ironworkers making weapons. The Kersal Moor meeting on 24 September had been followed by another Hartshead Moor meeting on 15 October, at which there was general talk of arming, whilst O'Connor came close to advocating tyrannicide. In Preston, on 5 November, he repeated similar views, and carried the argument also to the normally more peaceful Chartists of Scotland early in the New Year. Stephens was arrested in December, though immediately released on bail. A subscription for his defence raised over £1,000.

The delegates finally assembled at the British Hotel, Cockspur Street, in London on 4 February 1839. There were in all fifty-three of them, but, as normally a few were absent from sittings, their numbers did not exceed the fifty prohibited by one of the Six Acts of 1819. Some delegates had been chosen to represent several constituencies, preference being shown to London men who would have fewest expenses, and this latter group comprised a quarter of the whole. The LWMA monopolised London's own representation, with seven delegates. By far the largest contingent represented the industrial North, with twenty delegates, including O'Connor. Scotland sent eight, Birmingham five, the Midlands

hosiery districts three, and Wales two. The remaining delegates represented more isolated pockets of Chartism in England, such as Bristol, but only one, George Loveless (one of the celebrated Tolpuddle Martyrs), was named for an agricultural district, and he never took his seat (**36, 37, 64**).

By no means all the delegates were themselves of the working classes. Only John Collins belonged to that category in the Birmingham delegation. Richard Marsden, a handloom weaver from Preston, was no more typical than Lawrence Pitkethly, a prosperous draper from Huddersfield (**61**). In all, only about half the delegates could be called 'working men', and there was even one clergyman, Dr Wade from Warwick. The gathering was a sober and, as yet, dignified one [**doc. 5**]. Lovett was elected secretary, after Dr Wade had opened with prayers, and the meeting was told that the petition had now been signed by over half a million people.

After two days the Convention moved to nearby Bolt Court, Fleet Street, and settled down to discuss and prepare for the presentation of the petition. But for so many outspoken and strong-willed people to meet in the same room at the same time was a recipe for trouble, and it was not long in coming. Was the Convention merely to concern itself with the Petition, or was it to act as a proper People's Parliament? J. P. Cobbett, son of William Cobbett, argued the former, was defeated, and resigned. Should Chartists oppose the Anti-Corn Law League? O'Brien proposed that they should and the delegates agreed, but the men of Birmingham began to withdraw as the language of delegates, inside and outside the Convention, grew more violent. Was physical force to be contemplated? This question caused deep divisions, with O'Connor leading the militants. Above all, the delegates were divided over what to do next. Should they sit tight in London and wait, or rouse the country; and what should they do if Parliament rejected the Petition [**doc. 4**]?

These questions, and others of minor importance, occupied the delegates throughout the spring. Some drifted home or went on lecture tours to win more signatures, and to relieve their own sense of frustration. The Harney group made further progress in London with the foundation of a penny unstamped, the *Democrat*, in April, but overall London proved to be a lukewarm centre for fiery radicals accustomed to the fervour of the North [**doc. 8**]. Even Birmingham was growing more extreme, and the Attwood group was temporarily pushed out by extremists like J. P. Fussell and

John Powell (**63a, 71**). But as violence became more pronounced during the spring of 1839, so the government began to respond to the pleas of alarmed magistrates. John Frost, delegate for Newport and himself a JP, lost his commission of the peace in March; Vincent was arrested; Major General Sir Charles Napier (himself a Chartist sympathiser from the West Country) was put in charge of 6,000 troops in the Northern District; drilling by Chartists was prohibited (**86**).

On 7 May the National Petition was ready to be presented: it was three miles long and contained 1,280,000 signatures. However, Thomas Attwood, who was to have presented the Petition with John Fielden, was unhappy at the idea that if the Charter became law the Irish would get 200 of the 600 seats proposed for the new House of Commons. On the same day Lord Melbourne's government resigned and the 'Bedchamber Crisis' began. Fearing further arrests, particularly if a Conservative ministry were formed, the Convention transferred itself to Birmingham, where its thirty-five surviving delegates reassembled on 13 May in the Owenites' Lawrence Street Chapel. Here the Convention drew up a list of 'ulterior measures' – withdrawal of bank deposits (as had been threatened in May 1832), a 'sacred month' (as advocated by William Benbow in 1833), exclusive dealing (to put pressure on shopkeepers) – which were to be put to the people if the petition were rejected. Amid further arrests the Convention then adjourned while feeling was tested in the country. Mass meetings were again held, on Newcastle Town Moor (20 May), Hartshead Moor (21 May) and Kersal Moor (25 May) [**doc. 7**]. Further arrests occurred, and remaining moderates began to doubt the wisdom of the course along which violent demagogues like Dr. John Taylor and Peter McDouall were leading them. The Scots were reverting to their more traditional moderation, while even Feargus O'Connor's outspokenness concealed a certain ambiguity of meaning. The Convention reassembled in Birmingham on 1 July, and on the following day resolved to return to London in a week, but on 4 July a posse of police was brought in from London to clear a crowd in the Bull Ring (meetings there had been banned in May). The police clashed with the crowd, a riot broke out, troops were called in, and Taylor and McDouall were arrested [**doc. 9**]. With the trouble continuing the following day, Lovett raised the matter in the Convention. Although himself opposed to violence, he proposed resolutions criticising the authorities and deploring the arrests [**doc. 10**]. The resolutions were then placarded in the streets over his name. Immediately Lovett was arrested, together with John Collins, who had taken the resolutions to the printer.

Harried by further arrests, the Convention then returned to London, and on 12 July Attwood and Fielden proposed that the House of Commons consider the Petition. Disraeli was one of those who spoke in favour (putting the case which he was to present so persuasively in his novel, *Sybil*), but the motion failed by 235 votes to 46.

The Chartists' bluff was now called, though the number of votes cast for (thirteen) and against (six) the 'sacred month' shows how far the Convention had fallen in leadership and importance. Realism set in. The industrial districts were not ready for, or prepared to, strike. O'Connor, supported by O'Brien, succeeded in reversing the vote: the paper tiger had roared; now the government was to move on to the offensive. The Convention was prorogued on 6 August, and finally dissolved a month later by its remaining twenty-three delegates (**7, 37**).

With the rejection of the Petition and the collapse of the Convention, Chartism as a movement was in danger of disintegration. So long as the political strategy had seemed to offer hope, the leaders, however violent their speeches, could exert some kind of control over the movement, but, as the autumn of 1839 turned to winter, local initiatives for direct action came to the fore. Plans for a concerted strike gave way to plans for a concerted rising. How far such plans got is uncertain. Rumours were rife in the West Riding in the late autumn, but only in South Wales did anything happen.

Here, on the night of 3/4 November, some 7,000 colliers and iron-workers led by John Frost, Zephaniah Williams and William Jones, marched on Newport at the beginning of what was to have been a concerted rising in the Valleys to capture key towns and establish a republic. But despite widespread mobilisation, the March on Newport was mismanaged and the attack on the town did not take place until after day-break. After a short but fierce battle at the Westgate Hotel, the Chartists were dispersed by a few dozen soldiers. Twenty-four people were killed or died from their injuries (more than twice the death toll at 'Peterloo'), 125 were arrested, and 21 people were charged with high treason, including Frost, Williams and Jones (**73, 73a**). A special commission began to hear the cases in Monmouth on 10 December [**docs 11, 12**]. So ended the most celebrated armed rebellion of the nineteenth century in Britain, but its failure did nothing in the short term to reduce the political temperature. Chartists planned, or were reported to be planning, further risings in the event of Frost's conviction. A government spy named James Harrison was active in the West Riding, where a simultaneous rising was reported to be planned for 26 January, led by Robert Peddie of Edinburgh (who was believed by the Chartists – erroneously – to be a spy). The real leader in Bradford, Peter Bussey, had absented himself from meetings after Frost's arrest, and it is possible that Peddie was planning a real rising following the failure of similar attempts in Dewsbury and Sheffield earlier in the month, but it all came to nothing (**69**) [**doc. 15**].

Spring saw the complete rout of Chartism. Further arrests mopped up all potential pockets of resistance, and emigration removed other leaders (including Bussey). Frost and the other Newport leaders were condemned to death for treason but were transported for life instead. Samuel Holberry, the Sheffield leader, was sentenced to four years in March, and Peddie to three. Most of the national leaders, scores of local leaders, and hundreds of followers, were tried and imprisoned. Between June 1839 and June 1840 at least 543 Chartists were detained, for periods of between a few weeks and a few years. Lovett and Collins were sentenced to twelve months in August 1839, and Stephens to eighteen months. In February O'Brien was sentenced also to eighteen months, as was O'Connor in March. Harney was one of the few to escape, when a Grand Jury refused to indict him for one of his milder speeches in March.

The first stage in the history of Chartism was now over, with the men who had shaped its origins safely locked away, learning the errors of their ways. Chief of these appeared to be lack of organisation. The Convention had been elected not by branch societies but by mass meetings. Now rebuilding was to begin, with greater emphasis on local organisation, local objects and local men, while never losing sight of the overall national ambition to secure the People's Charter.

4 1840–1847: New Moves and New Hopes

Chartism up to 1840 had been shaped largely by its leaders and the movements in which they had previously been involved, Lovett, Oastler, Attwood and Stephens variously adding radicalism, populism and a dash of Old Testment moral indignation. Despite the tensions between these elements, Chartism had united rather than divided the movement of protest. Now the reality of the divisions was to reassert itself as different leaders sought their own ways forward. But what had been achieved up to 1840 was not immediately lost. The will to work for the common goal, the Charter, was still there, and in 1842 the events of 1839 were to be largely repeated.

The first step in reorganisation came in Scotland in August 1839, when delegates met in Glasgow to promote Chartist propaganda. A weekly periodical, the *Chartist Circular*, was begun and a committee formed with the title 'Universal Suffrage Central Committee for Scotland' (**72, 72a**). One of the lecturers employed by the Scots was Harney, who soon began to turn his mind to a similar project for England. Next, in London, Hetherington started a Metropolitan Charter Union (April 1840), and O'Connor from gaol floated his ideas in the *Northern Star*. On 20 July 1840 a conference of twenty-three delegates gathered in Manchester to form a new Chartist organisation for England. The outcome was the National Charter Association, which was to constitute the backbone of Chartist organisation for the next dozen years. The NCA was intended to be a federation of local branches, but, as this was contrary to the Corresponding Societies Act, the theory was abandoned, and instead each locality put forward its own nominees for the general council which thereby became an undivided body of several hundred members. Not only did this keep the NCA within the law; the lists of local names printed in the *Northern Star* give the historian the best evidence as to the occupations of Chartist members in the localities (**38**).

During 1841, local Chartist and Working Men's Associations were drawn into the NCA, especially under its revised, legal, consti-

29

tution. By December 1841 there were 282 localities with 13,000 members; by April 1842, 50,000 members and 401 localities were being claimed. The NCA was blessed by O'Connor, who sought from gaol to influence its policy and to keep himself to the forefront through his columns in the *Northern Star*, but as it and Chartism expanded even it was unable to encompass all Chartist energies. Indeed, the association of the NCA with O'Connor was sufficient to ensure the existence of rivals, most notably in London where Lovett, released in July 1840, began to implement his scheme for a National Association; and in Scotland, where no Scottish local-ities joined the NCA until 1843 (**72**). In June 1841 there had been probably no more than 5,000 NCA members, whereas the previous month a petition for Frost's release had contained two million signatures (**37**).

At the end of August 1841, Feargus O'Connor, 'the lion of freedom', came from his den in York Castle gaol [**doc. 17**]. Char-tism's most dynamic leader was again free and able to breathe life into what he considered to be *his* movement. In triumph he toured the country, feeding his enormous sense of self-importance on the cheers and congratulations of his loyal subjects. At one such meeting in Birmingham in September, Peter McDouall proposed a plan for another National Petition and Convention. The NCA took up the proposal, and plans went ahead for a Convention to meet in London in February (later deferred to April) 1842.

Despite the Chartist splits, both the elections and the petitioning were more competently organised than in 1839. Members of the Convention were chosen not by mass meetings but by paid-up members of the NCA. This involved a much smaller number of people – O'Connor, for example, topping the poll of West Riding delegates with only 1,741 votes. Nevertheless, 3,317,752 signatures were claimed for the Petition, which T. S. Duncombe presented to the House of Commons on 2 May. The House debated whether to hear the Chartists or not, before easily deciding not to by 287 votes to 49. As in 1839, the months of preparation had led nowhere. Also, as in 1839, the economic position of the country, which had deteriorated again in 1841, plunged into the depths of severe industrial depression. The Chartists had to reconsider their tactics against a background of economic and social crisis.

The connection between the Chartists and the wave of strikes which swept the industrial districts in the summer of 1842 was then, as now, a subject of much controversy. The unrest began among the coal miners of Staffordshire in July 1842, and by

September fourteen English counties, eight Scottish and one Welsh (Glamorgan) had been affected by the unrest. The textile areas of Lancashire, Cheshire and Yorkshire lay at the heart of the trouble, and it is here that the evidence of Chartist involvement is strongest. The *Leeds Mercury*, mouth-piece of the West Riding liberal manufacturers, without hesitation headlined its report of events 'The Chartist Insurrection', though *The Times* and the *Northern Star* were less certain. Indeed, the industrial unrest seems to have caught the Chartist leaders unawares, and they were at first inclined to see it as an Anti-Corn Law League plot (**63e, 75, 76, 77, 78, 78a, 78b**).

The trouble began with the decision of the cotton masters of Ashton-under-Lyne and Stalybridge to reduce wages. Two of the firms involved then agreed under pressure from the weavers to take back the latest reductions, but Bayley Brothers at first refused, and on 5 August their workers struck, marched through the streets, and brought the whole of Ashton to a standstill. Two days later on Mottram Moor a mass meeting resolved on a general strike until the Charter became the law of the land, and on 8 August a meeting in Stalybridge resolved to turn out all the factories there and in neighbouring Dukinfield; and the following day the crowd marched on Manchester. After giving public assurances that no violence was intended, they were allowed to proceed and persuaded the trades of Manchester to join the strike. By 11 August over a hundred cotton factories, many dyeworks and machine shops, and about 50,000 workmen were idle. A conference of eighty trades delegates then assembled at the Carpenters' Hall, appealed for law and order, and endorsed the Charter. The strike then spread across the Pennines to Yorkshire, with gangs of strikers pulling out the boiler plugs to put out the fires and halt the works, while in Manchester the trades delegates continued to meet [**doc. 22**].

By coincidence, the Executive of the NCA was also in Manchester on 16 August, to unveil a statue to Henry Hunt on the anniversary of 'Peterloo'. The reaction of these leaders is instructive, for, although individual members of the NCA were involved in the strike, it is clear that the majority of the Executive had been caught by surprise. William Hill, editor of the *Northern Star*, and Harney actually opposed McDouall's motion that the NCA give official support to the strike, but the majority followed O'Connor in seizing the opportunity to show Chartist solidarity with the trades delegates. This was far from the 'Plug Plot' becoming a 'Chartist Plot', however.

31

So why did he do so?
To get workers on side.

This is mirrored in O'Connor's thinking that you should write a Chartism

On the other side, despite the vote of two-thirds of the trades delegates in Manchester to support the Charter, voting in other places was not so clearly in favour, for the Manchester trades were not wholly typical of the textile areas. The workers of Stockport, Macclesfield, Stalybridge, Mossley, Lees and Bury preferred to restrict the issue to one of wages, and the cotton spinners of Oldham were one group to decide against supporting the Charter. Yet there was a considerable support for Chartism among the strikers, even amongst those who preferred to keep political and economic issues apart.

Indeed, this is the real significance of the 1842 strikes, for they show the close personal connections at local levels between trade union and political activists, quite apart from any official 'no politics' rule in the unions. The events of 1842 enable historians to glimpse the extent to which local radicals were able to express the grievances of the workmen and make the association between economics and politics. In the depths of misery the fundamental unity of the working-class communities of the North was demonstrated, so that reporters with local knowledge could identify, as only patient historical research has been able to do since, the local trades leaders of 1842 as Chartists (**78**).

The extent and depth of violence in the summer of 1842 was greater than that of 1839, Newport excepted, and the activities of the strikers in Yorkshire certainly overshadow the abortive Bradford rising of 1840. Troops defending Akroyd's mill at Halifax clashed with the crowd come to draw the plugs, and prisoners were taken. (Akroyd had recently reduced wages by 20 per cent.) A rescue of the prisoners was attempted as the omnibus carrying them and the troops escorting them was attacked on the narrow road at Salterhebble. The ambush failed, the prisoners were safely brought to Elland station, but on the return journey stones were hurled from the housetops at the troops as they escorted a second omnibus carrying ordinary passengers to Halifax (**47d**). Ironically, one of the passengers injured in this way was the _Northern Star_ reporter! But such violence was sporadic and short-lived and, although the police and troops suffered setbacks, the final result could never be in doubt.

The strikes themselves were soon over. O'Connor came out against them in the _Northern Star_ about the same time as misery was forcing the men back to work. At a conference on 20 August, the trades delegates recommended a return to work. During September tension eased: the harvest of 1842 was a good one, and trade,

economic

HARVEST

which in July had begun to show signs of improvement, by October was sufficiently recovered for some employers to reconsider their attitude. In Ashton, where the trouble had started, they agreed to take back the reductions.

As in 1839–40, the authorities now struck hard at the leaders of the troubles. Arrests began in August soon after the NCA had endorsed the strikes. In October, 274 cases were tried in Staffordshire, 54 of the accused being transported and 154 imprisoned, including Thomas Cooper, who had been one of the most outspoken orators in favour of the strikers in the Potteries. He was sentenced to two years in prison, from which he was to emerge a changed man (**43**). McDouall went into self-imposed exile, but O'Connor was arrested and indicted for seditious conspiracy in September. His trial, along with that of fifty-eight others, opened at Lancaster on 1 March 1843. They were found guilty on a number of lesser charges, after a favourable summing up by the judge, and when the counsel for the defence sued for a writ of error on the grounds of a faulty indictment, the prisoners were released and never called up for sentence (**54a**). But by 1843 there was less need for harshness. The crisis was over, and was not to be known again on this scale until, with another downturn in the economy in 1847, the Chartists once more surged forward as a major threat to public order in 1848.

After 1842 the Chartist leadership completed that disintegration which it had been threatening to accomplish since 1839, and which had been apparent since 1840; while, at the local level, Chartists were left high and dry, a dedicated rump without an active mass following, who were to be most successful when they busied themselves with other things. Yet Chartism did not die, and the many personal and local directions into which the hopes of 1839 and 1842 were channelled remain important to the historian. To write Chartism off in 1842 is not only to render inexplicable the revival of 1848, but it is also to undervalue the whole Chartist experience [**doc. 33**] (**63f**).

Different leaders followed different ways: Lovett placed his emphasis on education, while Vincent and Lowery took up the cause of temperance; Christian Chartism appealed to Chartists in Scotland and Birmingham; and Feargus O'Connor devoted himself increasingly to the land question. Other diversions came in the form of trade union activity, Owenite Socialism, the Anti-Corn Law League and foreign affairs, while some groups turned with some success to involvement in local government.

33

William Lovett's 'new move' was worked out by him and John Collins while they were in Warwick gaol, and their ideas were published in 1840 under the title *Chartism; A New Organisation for the People, embracing a plan for the Education and Improvement of the People, politically and socially.* There was little in the work that was new, and it contains echoes of both the National Union of the Working Classes and the London Working Men's Association, with its plan for 'The National Association of the United Kingdom, For Promoting the Political and Social Improvement of the People' [**doc. 25**]. The scheme was denounced by the *Northern Star*, though this merely confirmed the mutual suspicion which existed between the Lovett and O'Connor groups. Lovett's old London colleagues, Hetherington and Watson, as well as Francis Place, were more favourably inclined, and London was to see the only district association (1841) to be commenced along lines intended in the book for every district. The National Association Hall in Holborn was opened in 1842, but further progress was slow; a Sunday school was begun in 1843, and gradually Lovett was able to make it a centre for his educational and other schemes until it closed in 1857 (**42**). But during this time he passed from the centre of the Chartist stage. After 1842 he had broken with the movement he had created, though he never despaired of the cause or of the peaceful means by which he believed success alone could be achieved (**57**).

These views were also shared by Henry Vincent, whose imprisonment had been a cause of the Newport rising, and Robert Lowery, who had been one of the outspoken leaders from Tyneside. Though Vincent was active in the National Association, both he and Lowery were prepared for even more co-operation with middle-class radicals, and their chosen means of moral reformation was the Temperance movement. At first Vincent sought to unite Chartism and Temperance as Teetotal Chartism, a move condemned by O'Connor and which survived for less than a year [**doc. 27**]. By 1842 Vincent, like Lovett, was passing out of Chartism and more directly into alliance with the middle classes. In such men as he and Lowery we can see the origins of mid-nineteenth-century popular liberalism as a moral concept which was to secure the loyalty of the Victorian artisan for Mr Gladstone. Although O'Connor was not opposed to temperance as such, he was firmly against any new moves which would detract from that pure Chartism which he identified with himself (**58, 59, 59a, 95**).

He adopted the same attitude to religious Chartism, which he fiercely denounced in the *Northern Star* not so much because he was

34

an infidel as because he saw it to be an irrelevancy [**doc. 27**]. Yet to many Chartists, especially in Scotland, religion was central [**doc. 26**]. The local leader in Paisley, the Reverend Patrick Brewster, was a Presbyterian minister, and from 1840 one of the most prominent Chartists in Glasgow was Arthur O'Neil, a professional lecturer on political, scientific and religious subjects, who in June was appointed full-time missionary for the Lanarkshire Universal Suffrage Association. Each Sunday he preached to congregations of Chartists. By the beginning of 1841 there were at least twenty Chartist Churches in Scotland, with regular preaching services in all in about thirty localities (**62g, 72, 72a**). O'Neil himself, who was half English, then accepted an invitation to Birmingham from John Collins, who had also been a local preacher and Sunday school teacher before his Chartist days. Here O'Neil founded an active Chartist Church and conducted services in West Bromwich and other Midland towns, before his arrest in 1842 and sentence at the Stafford trials to a year in prison (**80, 80a, 81**).

Those who were not attracted to religion could, and did, move in other directions – towards Owenism, for example. The Owenites themselves had rapidly expanded in the late 1830s as they converted public opinion in preparation for the commencement of their own particular millennium: their community at Queenwood Farm in Hampshire. Like the Chartists they had their local meetings, and in many places shared a common core of local leaders with the Chartists. During the heady days of 1839 the Chartists probably picked up a great deal of experienced, ideologically committed leadership from the ranks of Owen's followers, but after 1842 some of these began to transfer their energies back. As with educational, temperance and religious Chartism, the appeal of Owenism was to moral regeneration. Men like Joshua Hobson and John Ardill of the *Northern Star*, Lawrence Pitkethly of Huddersfield and Isaac Ironside of Sheffield were equally at home in both movements, not to mention Hetherington and Watson who, unlike Lovett, returned to their Owenite roots in the 1840s (**32**).

This is understandable. Less easy to follow is the appeal of foreign affairs, by which is meant not just the customary interest in European republicanism to which Harney devoted much of his time in the mid-1840s, but also the more complex and mysterious influence of David Urquhart. The latter was a Tory ex-diplomat, who believed that Lord Palmerston was a Russian spy because he seemed prepared to betray Turkey to the Russians. Such nonsense had great appeal, for Russia was cordially hated by all radicals as the oppressor of Poland and of all European liberties. Urquhart was convinced that the Russians had penetrated to the very heart of the Chartist movement itself, and he persuaded Thomas Doubleday (editor of the *Northern Liberator*), and Lowery of this in 1840 (**91**). For once O'Connor was right to see the damage being done to the cause, though Urquhartism itself was no more a plot against Chartism than Chartism was a Russian plot.

The principal campaigner against Urquhart's views, and the upholder of a true republican interest in foreign affairs, was George Julian Harney. Since 1840, when he had been acquitted by a Grand Jury, Harney had worked to create Chartist organisation in Sheffield and, although never a moderate, his tactical thinking was against the strike movement of 1842. Nevertheless, he was arrested with O'Connor, but like him was never brought to sentence. He then moved closer to the O'Connor circle, and in 1843 was appointed sub-editor of the *Northern Star* and a member of the NCA executive. He met Friedrich Engels at the *Northern Star* office in Leeds, and through him became acquainted with a number of foreign republican exiles who had made England, chiefly London, their temporary home. In 1844, following a visit from the German communist, Wilhelm Weitling, some refugees, together with Owenites and Chartists of the Lovett school, had formed the Democratic Friends of All Nations, and three years later the same London group of liberals founded the People's International League, which was to set a precedent for a number of similar broadly-based middle- and working-class republican societies in the 1850s, as well as for the revival of moderate Chartism in London in 1848 (**32**). Harney was not of this group, but in 1845, at a dinner held on 22 September to celebrate the first French Republic of 1792, a more extreme party emerged under the title of Fraternal Democrats, which rapidly became the focus for English, German and Polish socialists, including Marx, Engels, Karl Schapper, Harney, and a newcomer to British radicalism, Ernest Jones. Though Harney was careful to reassure the NCA that the Fraternal Democrats was not a rival body, undoubtedly the energies put into the cause of foreign republicanism were at the expense of the domestic movement. Characteristically O'Connor saw the danger, and in a xenophobic article in the *Northern Star* in 1847 he urged his followers to have 'nothing whatever to do with any foreign movement' (**90**).

Yet O'Connor may well have been confusing cause with effect. The readiness with which leaders took up other causes did contribute to the decline of Chartism, but these diversions were also the product of that decline. Chartism had failed in the strategy of 1839 and 1842, and imprisonment had left no doubts in the minds of many Chartists as to where real power lay in the state. With the end of the industrial depression the fires of passion had cooled. The dedicated leaders had to find some compensating activities, but their followers were conspicuously unmoved.

The most fruitful area into which some Chartists turned was local government. What they had failed to achieve at Westminster they were at least to sample in local government in such places as Leeds and Sheffield, led by Joshua Hobson and Isaac Ironside respectively. The latter had organised a system of ward committees, which in 1848 were able to put forward seven successful candidates in the Town Council elections; by the following November there were twenty-two nominally Chartist members on the council, and Ironside was able to raise a discussion at Council meetings on such topics as the Charter and national secular education. His success is attributable partly to his personality and the radical traditions of Sheffield, and partly to the household suffrage franchise which made democratic participation in local government a real possibility (**69a**).

In Leeds, the Chartist attack began at vestry meetings at which improvement commissioners were elected. Hobson stood in 1840 and was defeated, but a fellow Chartist, John Jackson, was successful. Two years later the Chartists captured control of the vestry and carried their full list of nineteen candidates. A new improvement Act then did away with the system of electing improvement commissioners, so the Chartists turned their attention to the town council. They also had success with the annual election of churchwardens, carrying the complete lists for 1842–45 and working amicably with the vicar, W. F. Hook, who was a firm friend of the factory movement. The 1842 municipal elections, however, were not a success, but ward organisation was concentrated on the working-class Hunslet and Holbeck wards and, in 1843, Jackson and Hobson were both elected for Holbeck, with Hobson top of the poll. At no time were the Chartists in Leeds able to build up the kind of party which Ironside did in Sheffield, but until 1853 there were Chartists on Leeds Town Council, with a peak of seven councillors in 1849–50 (**62b**). Their chief value was nuisance value, but they nevertheless represented for Chartism a greater measure of success than their one electoral victory at the national level, the victory of O'Connor at Nottingham in the 1847

Development

general election: he made even less impact on the political system than the local councillors. Success at the polls, local or national, was bound to be of a limited nature without universal suffrage, yet without such success how was the Charter to be achieved?

On a broader stage, the question of strategy introduced two further distractions which were probably more important than any others. The first was the return to purely economic agitation by the trades societies, a fact recognised in the policy of the *Northern Star*, which adopted as its sub-title on 30 November 1844 '*and National Trades Journal*'. This was an attempt to broaden the basis of the readership of the paper and admits to the existence of a growing trade union body which was not specifically Chartist. The first important trade union to be set up in the 1840s was the Miners' Association, founded in 1841, which by 1844 was said to have a membership of 100,000 from nearly all the coalfields of Great Britain. The Association appointed as its legal advisor William Prowting Roberts, who was shortly to be associated also with Feargus O'Connor. The Union engaged in a bitter strike in 1844, which failed disastrously, and its doings were closely followed in the *Northern Star* in 1844 and 1845. The latter year saw a renewed attempt at a more general organisation of unionists, the National Association of United Trades for the Protection of Labour, which owed a great deal to its first president, the radical MP, T. S. Duncombe. The depression of 1847–48 destroyed the Miners' Association and weakened the National Association of United Trades, but did give the Ten Hours Movement its chance at last to secure a further Factory Act (**35, 88a**). Such concern with the more immediate needs of working men suggests an important alternative to the Chartist programme in the mid-1840s.

The second approach, easier in good times than in bad, was to merge Chartism with similar progressive movements among the middle classes, chiefly with the Complete Suffrage Union and the Anti-Corn Law League. The CSU itself was shortlived. It represented those forces of moderation which Attwood's BPU had stood for before the violence of 1839, and was announced in Birmingham in January 1842 by Joseph Sturge, a Quaker free-trader and Birmingham alderman. By April, over fifty local Complete Suffrage Associations had been formed and a petition was presented to Parliament in what appeared to be an attempt to rival the parallel activities of the NCA. Although the CSU was supported mainly by anti-O'Connorites like Lovett, Vincent,

Lowery and Collins, O'Connor too could see the advantages of a middle-class tactical alliance. In the 1841 general election he had urged Chartists to support Tories, which precipitated a breach with O'Brien, but in a by-election at Nottingham in August 1842 he threw his support behind Sturge against John Walter of *The Times*, even though Walter was a longstanding opponent of the new poor law. But this did not mean that Sturge had won the Chartists over, as the CSU discovered at its December conference when the price of Chartist support was named as the Charter itself. Both Lovett and O'Connor, while remaining hostile to each other, refused to accept a 'New Bill of Rights' in place of the Charter. The temporary alliance was broken. Some Chartists, like Vincent, joined the CSU; others, like Lovett, pursued their own courses. The only party to gain were the O'Connorites who were now firmly in control of the NCA (**37, 38a**).

The question of the relation between the Chartists and the middle-class radicals of the Anti-Corn Law League was more complicated, as working-class attitudes to the Corn Laws themselves were divided. Some, possibly most, opposed them as the cause of high bread prices, though they also thought Corn Law repeal, without the Charter, would be meaningless. This was O'Brien's view. Others, such as spokesmen for the textile areas like James Leach, argued that without a Ten Hours Bill the benefits of repeal would not accrue to the working classes. And at times O'Connor led others in being out-and-out protectionist, seeing the strength of the agricultural interest as essential to the well-being of the labour force. Just as the Birmingham background to Chartism was likely to aid the CSU, so the Manchester background was likely to discourage any brotherly co-operation between the Chartists and the League, and between 1839 and 1842 the history of the two movements is largely one of friction and mistrust, as the League tried to win working-class support [**doc. 23**]. And, as with the CSU, breakdown in relations came in the depths of the 1842 depression. Thereafter the decline in unemployment and a fall in the price of bread eased the worst social tensions, and clashes between the two groups ceased as the League restricted itself to more middle-class meetings and missionary activities among the tenant farmers (**33**). Moderate Chartists began to advocate Corn Law repeal. At Northampton, in 1844, Cobden debated the subject with O'Connor, and at last won him over to the cause of repeal and co-operation with sympathetic radicals among the middle classes (**94**). Though Harney at the *Northern Star* remained suspicious of Whigs, the editorial tribute paid to Peel on proposing repeal in 1846 is a remarkable witness to the distance travelled by the Chartists since 1842.

The story of Chartism between 1842 and 1848 can be told in a way which presents O'Connor as the hero – the man whose constancy to the cause when others turned away showed him to be the most perceptive of all the Chartists (**54a**). This case can be made, despite the *volte face* over the Corn Laws, and should not be so readily dismissed as some historians since Gammage have been inclined to do, but any such assessment has to take into consideration O'Connor's involvement in the greatest distraction of all – the Land Plan.

The thinking behind the Land Plan does not seem to have been directly political, though the Anti-Corn Law League did use land settlement to create 'faggot' votes. O'Connor was creating not voters but tenants, and his plan was too conservative for much of the English radical leadership. Although some of O'Connor's earliest land speeches, on 'The land and its capabilities' and 'What is the remedy for our grievances?' were delivered at the Owenite Hall of Science in Manchester (March 1842), this had more to do with the size of the auditorium than the closeness of O'Connor's ideas to Owen's. The latter advocated communities for the transformation of society, and looked forward to the golden age; O'Connor advocated individual tenancies, and looked back to the golden age. The latter was the more attractive, though both proved to be equally impracticable.

The Land Plan nevertheless produced a hearty response among the English working classes in both town and country, for it showed not so much O'Connor's Irish roots (**54**) as his profound grasp of English radical tradition. The land – in a view which went back to the writings of Thomas Paine and Thomas Spence, and beyond them to the Levellers and the Diggers of the seventeenth century – was the guarantee of individual freedom from political oppression and economic exploitation. More immediately, access to the land would bring direct relief to labourers still suffering in the towns, as the *Northern Star* explained in 1843 [**doc. 28**].

The land question was mentioned at Chartist Conventions in 1843 and 1844, and finally in 1845 the Chartist Co-operative Land Society was approved by the annual NCA Convention meeting in London. The proposal was for the Society to purchase lands which it would then rent out to subscribers at £5 per annum for a two-acre allotment. This would yield sufficient profit for more lands to be purchased and so on until (as with Owen's plan) the existing arrangements of society would be overtaken by the new. The fully-fledged plan was presented to a special conference held in Manchester in December 1845, and the ballot for the first tenants was held the following Easter. Undeterred by the refusal of the Registrar of Friendly Societies to issue a certificate to the Land Society, O'Connor renamed it the Chartist Land Co-operative Company and proceeded at speed. Enthusiasm mounted, not least because the use of the ballot promised instant salvation to the lucky few. The first estate, at Heronsgate (renamed O'Connorville) near Watford, was acquired in March 1846 and advertised in the *Northern Star* the following May. A second ballot was held, and at the end of the year a Land and Labour Bank was launched to gather funds. Legal complications were already apparent. The Bank could not be run by the Company and so had to be administered by O'Connor himself, and the Company was never actually registered as a joint stock company. Despite O'Connor's own legal qualifications and his employing W. P. Roberts to act on the Company's behalf, the whole affair rapidly degenerated into legal chaos. As an MP, O'Connor applied for special legislation to enable him to operate within the terms of the Friendly Societies Acts, and the House of Commons appointed a Select Committee to enquire into the Company. The problem was whether the scheme fell foul of any, or indeed all, of the Friendly Societies, Lotteries, Bank and Joint Stock Acts. The complications were driving O'Connor literally mad, and, when the Lord Chief Justice ruled out all hope of the Joint Stock Acts being applied in 1850, O'Connor petitioned Parliament for a Bill to dissolve the Company, which was finally done in August 1851 (**83b**).

The extent of these legal problems only gradually became apparent to the wider Chartist body, and, indeed, to most readers of the *Northern Star* the initial picture had seemed very bright [**doc. 29**]. A second estate, at Lowbands in Worcestershire, was acquired in August 1847, two months after the opening of O'Connorville on May Day. Three more villages were to follow, at Minster Lovell (renamed Charterville) in Oxfordshire, at Snig's End in Gloucestershire and at Great Dodford in Worcestershire. In all, over £100,000 was collected from some 70,000 subscribers, although only 250 of them were actually settled on the land. The drive behind the successful appeal of the Land Plan was depression. The villages were opened at the same time as unemployment was again rising in the wake of the 1847 commercial crisis and the bad harvest across Europe. Between December 1846 and August 1847 nearly £50,000 was subscribed, and in the full year of 1847 about 600 branches of the Land Company were formed (**92, 93**). But, with the depression also came revolution in Europe, and a return to more traditional forms of Chartist agitation in Britain.

5 1848–1858: Reconciliation to Defeat

Chartist minds turned to politics again with the general election of 1847, at which Feargus O'Connor became the first and last purely Chartist Member of Parliament. Then came a commercial crisis, following the bad wheat harvest of 1846 and the bad potato harvests of 1846 and 1847, which brought political systems tumbling across Europe. The *Northern Star*, already excited by the Cracow rising of 1846, reported the 'springtime of the peoples' with unconcealed delight. Harney and Jones, Hetherington and W. J. Linton – the whole spectrum of Chartist opinion – celebrated the events, from the Paris revolution of February, through the fall of Metternich, to the rising of the Hungarians. Hardly a European country seemed exempt, and Britain was to be no exception [**doc. 34**].

The general election of July 1847 resulted in the return of a weak Whig government led by Lord John Russell, but the new Chartist campaign did not really get under way until the winter. Then a combination of events in France and Ireland gave republican Chartists like Harney and Jones new heart. Links were established with Smith O'Brien and John Mitchel of the Irish Confederation, and O'Connor could at last feel that his dream of a united radical movement on both sides of the Irish Sea was about to be fulfilled under his leadership. The political crisis in France was eagerly followed in England; meetings were held in London to support O'Connor (whose election to Parliament was being challenged), and to commemorate the Cracow rising of 1846; and, when Louis Philippe's regime fell on 24 February, 1848, further meetings were called to congratulate the people of France. As in the rest of Europe, this latter event gave republicans everywhere the heart to try to do likewise. Meetings flowed out of doors, and the Chartist orators again felt the warmth of large and enthusiastic crowds.

On 6 March, a middle-class meeting in Trafalgar Square to demand the repeal of the income tax, was declared illegal, but was taken over by the Chartists with G. W. M. Reynolds in the chair. Reynolds was a republican journalist who had predicted the fall of Louis Philippe in the *Weekly Dispatch*, and was better known as a writer than a speaker. Up to this point he had hardly been a prominent Chartist, and it is not certain how far the events which followed can specifically be described as 'Chartist'. After the meeting the crowd remained on the streets and was dispersed only with difficulty by the police. That evening, some of the crowd marched to Buckingham Palace, smashing lamps and windows on the way. For three days the mobs ran free in London and, though no real threat was posed, the Queen and her ministers took the matter seriously in view of the contemporary revolutions in Europe (**65, 89a**).

On the same day as Reynolds chaired the meeting in London, disturbances also occurred in Glasgow, again for reasons more economic than political. Crowds of hungry unemployed workers marched through the streets of Glasgow with shouts of 'Bread or revolution'. When looting began the troops were called in and five people were shot. In Manchester the following day a crowd of youths tried to storm the Union work-house, but was dispersed by the police after a four-hours' struggle. The police station in Oldham Road was attacked, lamps were smashed, and for three days the rioting continued, the crowd using fragments of broken market stalls as weapons against the police. Calm was eventually restored without recourse to troops: this was a riot, not the beginning of a Revolution, and there was no avowed link between the rioters and the Charter. Indeed, the Chartist leader, James Leach, disowned the rioters. At the height of these troubles, on 6 March, O'Connor visited the Potteries, scene of some of the worst rioting in 1842, where he was greeted by a crowd of several thousands, but there was no trouble.

The following week, on Kennington Common in South London, possibly 20,000 people gathered, along with some 4,000 police; and right across the country similar mass meetings were held to hear speeches from such national leaders as Jones and O'Connor, and local men like Samuel Kydd, George White and Joseph Barker in the West Riding. On St Patrick's Day a fraternal meeting of Chartists and Irish, addressed by O'Connor, filled the Free Trade Hall in Manchester: the ghost of the Irish Anti-Corn Law League mob, which had smashed up O'Connor's lectures in Manchester in 1842, was finally laid [**docs 18, 19**]. Everywhere people were again proclaiming themselves for the Charter, and a new petition, to be presented by O'Connor, was gaining signatures by the thousand (**7, 37**).

In London, crowded meetings held in the headquarters of the Owenites, the John Street Institute, made plans for the presentation of the petition. On 4 April the Convention began to sit, and heard reports from its forty-seven delegates on the lamentable state of the country and the determination of the people to resist any further denial of their political rights. A peaceful rally was planned for Kennington Common on 10 April, to be followed by a procession to present the petition to the House of Commons. If the petition were rejected, the Queen would be called upon by an elected National Assembly to dissolve Parliament, and the Assembly would remain in session until a new government had agreed to make the Charter the law of the land. Public opinion in the capital was now very tense. Property-owners really seem to have feared that the Kennington Common meeting, despite its peaceful intentions, was to be the start of the English Revolution. Whether the government believed this seems very doubtful, but there were advantages in going along with the general feeling. The ministry was weak, but it could appear strong and give the impression of activity to its critics, and so claim the credit in retrospect. This said, even ministers must have had some doubts about how easy the Chartists would be to deal with. The Queen was safely at Osborne in the Isle of Wight, but Lord Palmerston was worried that the island's defences might not prove adequate. On 7 April the Chief Commissioner of Police banned the procession from Kennington Common, and the government began to rush a Security Bill through Parliament. The Duke of Wellington put himself forward to organise the defences of London, and special constables were enrolled in their thousands. The military was held in reserve, to be used only if the Chartists tried to cross the bridges towards Westminster. On 9 April Bronterre O'Brien advised against the meeting and resigned from the Convention (**65f**).

What followed has often been told. Crowds from all over London marched behind banners in their accustomed fashion, and assembled on Kennington Common where they were addressed by O'Connor. Estimates of the crowd vary, from half a million (O'Connor) and 150,000–170,000 (Gammage) to 12,000–15,000 (Lord John Russell). Russell was probably in the best position to know, though he may have played down the figure a little and not included sympathisers who did not actually reach the Common. The upper estimates could not physically have fitted on to the Common at all. O'Connor also claimed that 5,700,000 signatures had been appended to the petition, another exaggeration. He informed the crowd of the legal position and then advised his hearers to disperse. The petition was loaded into three cabs and taken off to Parliament, while O'Connor took another cab to the Home Office to assure Sir George Grey, the Home Secretary, of the legality of the day's proceedings. By 2 p.m. the Prime Minister was able to inform the Queen that the crisis was over [**doc. 35**].

This is not to say that Chartism was over, though contemporaries, followed by some historians, have written as though it were. 'Fiasco' is the word which springs to mind, but this is hardly appropriate, for even when Russell could write to the Queen that 'the Kennington Common Meeting has proved a complete failure' in the same letter he could add 'At Manchester, however, the Chartists are armed and have bad designs'. The sense of anticlimax after 10 April is more a measure of the fear (feigned or real) of the government, and of the very real scare which its supporters had experienced, than of the degree of Chartist failure. The subsequent attempt to portray the meeting and the petition as fiascos is as much ideological as historical. Chartism was made to look ridiculous, Chartists were made to feel ridiculous; their self-confidence was gradually undermined by the (largely retrospective) scorn of the propertied classes (**7, 65, 89a**).

Admittedly their tactics and O'Connor's antics gave grounds for this scorn. The petition was found to contain only 1,975,467 signatures, not nearly 6,000,000 as claimed, and doubts were cast on some of these. Yet this was hardly fair. The use of pseudonyms such as 'Victoria Rex', the 'Duke of Wellington' and 'Punch' should not necessarily be equated with forgery. Subscription lists to radical periodicals and 'victim funds' over the decades had abounded with such names, which nevertheless represented genuine people who either wanted to keep their identities private (for example, from their employers) or who wished to take the opportunity to 'cock a snook' at the authorities. The worthy parliamentary clerks had misread a traditional popular means of expression. Further doubt was cast on the authenticity of some signatures because they appeared in the same hand – evidence that Chartism was appealing to some of that 30 per cent of society who could not sign their own names, rather than of forgery. Nevertheless, even if the House of Commons did underestimate the number of petitioners, one cannot get near accepting O'Connor's figure as its true size.

On the day after the Kennington Common meeting, the Chartists resolved further action, and on 14 April the Convention supported a motion by Jones for a distribution of tracts to explain to the public the advantages which the Charter would confer, and a second motion by him for a memorial to the Queen. Preparations were set in train for summoning the National Assembly, and mass meetings were held in Scotland, England and Ireland. The country was by no means quiet: Aberdeen was thought to be in favour of forming a National Guard, the Chartists of Nottingham were arming themselves, and Ireland seethed on the edge of open rebellion. On the first of May the National Assembly met, but by this time the Chartist leadership was more fragmented than ever. O'Connor publicly announced his opposition, and Harney declined to take his seat in the Assembly. It had become very much Ernest Jones's affair. After two weeks of wrangling a Provisional Executive was appointed, led by Jones, after which the Assembly dissolved itself. Jones was undeterred, but he rightly realised that the Assembly did not have the mass support necessary for success (**53, 56**). London in 1848 was not Paris in 1789, nor even Paris in 1848. Harney's verdict in the *Northern Star*, written in November 1848, seems a just one: 'The errors of the "Convention" were enormously multiplied and magnified by the succeeding "Assembly"; and hence, what might have been a temporary repulse became a thorough defeat.'

Yet even this view could only be obtained from the perspective of the late autumn, the other side of a summer of discontent. The complacency of the government in April temporarily waned, and the severity of the punishments which followed the unrest was, if anything, greater than that displayed in 1839 and 1842. The Chartists may have contributed to their own defeat in April but in May and June it was the might of the government which finally put paid to their hopes. John Mitchel, the most extreme of the Irish Confederates, was sentenced on 24 May to fourteen years' transportation, and Smith O'Brien followed him in August after an attempted rising in Tipperary. Arming and drilling were widely reported in the West Riding in May, and on the 28th a crowd of 2,000 routed the police and special constables of Bradford, and troops had to be called in to restore order. 'If fighting with pluck against special constables and the police could make a revolution,' commented *The Times*, 'those who fought at Bradford ought to have succeeded.' The following day a massive silent march through the streets of London by an estimated 80,000 workers seemed to augur further troubles for the capital, and on 4 June meetings in the East End were broken up by the police on instructions from the Home

Office, precipitating a night of ugly street fighting. With a day of protest planned by the Provisional Executive for 12 June, the government had at last to act. This time, unlike 10 April, they were in deadly earnest. The leaders of the London meetings, including Jones, were arrested, and in a tense atmosphere heightened by the street fighting of the 'June Days' in Paris, he was sentenced to two years in prison. In 1848 he was an extreme republican and clear-sighted leader; when he emerged again in 1850 he was also a convinced socialist. But still the unrest continued. The London revolutionaries were divided into brigades and divisions, ready for a carefully planned uprising on 15 August [**doc. 36**]. In all only about a thousand men were involved, many of them Irish. Simultaneous risings were planned in the provinces, particularly in Lancashire, again involving a number of Irish. But the revolutionary cadre had been penetrated by government spies, and, as Harney appreciated, there was no mass support for these extreme activities. When the day of revolution came, the police were able to deal with the problems, and only in Ashton-under-Lyne, which rose a day early, did troops have to be called. The active leaders of violent Chartism were then arrested and sentenced. Many of them received two years or more; the revolution of 1848 in Britain was over (**7, 37, 44, 53, 56, 65, 89a, 97b**).

By this time, the violent wing of Chartism included very few of those who in 1839 had supported 'ulterior measures'. O'Connor, Harney and O'Brien, no less than Lovett, were not involved. Instead each had his own plans, and his own remnant to nurture.

On 22 March 1848 the London moderates who had first conceived the Charter more than ten years before met and formed the People's Charter Union, the object of which was 'by peaceable and legal means to obtain the People's Charter, as the great instrument for procuring those political and social reforms which are necessary for the well-being and progress of the Nation' (**106**). A few hundred people joined, and some of its members spent 10 April not on Kennington Common but watching the police for evidence of violence. The president of the Union was Thomas Cooper, and its members included James Watson, Henry Hetherington, G. J. Holyoake (a former Owenite and close friend of theirs) and W. J. Linton, a radical-republican engraver who was Mazzini's principal English admirer. Largely through the influence of Linton, the People's Charter Union concerned itself mainly with foreign affairs, and Holyoake and Linton ran a shortlived periodical entitled *The Cause of the People* in the heady days of May–July. William Lovett stood apart from this body and instead supported the People's League, founded at the National Hall on 24 April to unite middle- and working-class reformers. Its first secretary was Robert Lowery, but Lovett later took the post. As an organisation it made little headway and was dissolved the following year, but it was a sign of things to come (**42**). Between 1848 and 1858 the story of Chartism is largely that of a gradual coming to terms with reality. The Charter would never be achieved by a purely working-class agitation. When O'Connor spoke in favour of the Charter in the House of Commons in July 1849 he could collect only fourteen other supporters (**97**). The idea of an alliance with the middle classes, never far from the thoughts of the moderates, therefore increasingly came to appeal as the only realistic way forwards.

On Thomas Paine's birthday, 29 January 1849, a meeting, called by the indefatigable Francis Place at the Crown and Anchor Tavern, led to the formation of the National Parliamentary and Financial Reform Association, which sought to unite Manchester School radicals like Cobden and Bright, other middle-class radicals such as Joseph Hume and Sir Joshua Walmsley, MP for Leicester (who became president), with the moderate Chartists [**doc. 37**]. Their programme, devised by Hume and O'Connor, was for a 'Little Charter' of four points: household suffrage, the ballot, triennial parliaments and more equal distribution of seats (**98**). Also on Place's suggestion, the members of the People's Charter Union formed a Newspaper Stamp Abolition Committee, with Richard Moore as chairman and C. D. Collet as secretary. By amalgamation with other campaigns, this became in 1851 the Association for the Repeal of the Taxes on Knowledge, which successfully saw through the abolition of the compulsory penny stamp (1855) which Hetherington's earlier agitation had been unable to remove in 1836 (**32**).

'Unity is Strength' was the motto of these London radicals after 1848, but unity was hard to find. The more some groups allied with the middle classes, the harder it became for the different Chartist groups to come together. The main contending bodies in 1850, apart from the moderates of the People's Charter Union, were the National Reform League (followers of O'Brien), the Social Reform Union (followers of Robert Owen), and the by now much-divided NCA. In October 1850 an attempt was made to bring all these together in a National Charter and Social Reform Union, to advocate manhood suffrage, home colonisation (Owenite communities), limited liability for workmen's organisations (for co-operative schemes), a just poor law, freedom of speech and publication, and a national system of secular education. Although this was a programme which broadly represented working-class radical opinion, the attempt to bring so many idiosyncratic and diverse leaders together suceeded only in uniting them against the plan. The best hope of united action in fact lay with the old NCA, which still survived in a much attenuated form. In the Executive elections of December 1850, G. W. M. Reynolds topped the poll with 1,805 votes, followed by Harney (1,774), and Jones (1,757). O'Connor was seventh with only 1,314 votes, followed by Holyoake with 1,021. Some members of this ill-assorted crew, led by Holyoake, wanted to co-operate with the middle-class advocates of Hume's 'Little Charter'; others, notably Harney and Jones, did not. In April 1851 the Executive decided on a compromise policy of maintaining the distinctness of Chartism but of allowing individuals to co-operate with other, less radical bodies. The leaders then went on their customary lecture tours, but the disillusionment of another defeat, accompanied by an improvement in the economy, meant that the days of the mass meetings were over (**89**). In December 1851 Harney refused to stand for election to the Executive, and Jones, who was elected (he topped the poll with only 900 votes), refused to take his seat. With O'Connor confirmed mad in June 1852, the NCA had lost all its prestige. Seriously in debt it disappeared from the pages of history (**37, 97, 98**). As the *Star* newspaper (which had just replaced the old *Northern Star*) commented on 20 April 1852: 'The Charter is no more to be had *now* by asking for, than next year's apples are – like them they must grow and ripen first.'

Such Chartism as remained lay fallow, ready to be cultivated by individual gardeners with the patience to wait for a distant harvest, notably Jones, Harney and O'Brien.

With Jones in prison till 1850, it was Harney who took the lead until he parted company with O'Connor and the *Northern Star* in August 1850 over his extreme interest in foreign affairs which O'Connor believed to detract from the main business in hand. Harney's catholicity in fact was both his strength and his weakness. In October 1849 he tried to organise the Fraternal Democrats to infiltrate the NCA and by the time Jones was released in July 1850 he had largely been successful, grafting a programme of socialism on to the Charter. The Red Flag had replaced the Green Flag of the 1840s. As 'Howard Morton' (possibly the pseudonym for Helen MacFarlane) wrote in Harney's periodical, the *Red Republican*, in June 1850:

> Chartism in 1850 is a different thing from Chartism in 1840. The leaders of the English Proletarians have proved that they are true Democrats, and no shams, by going ahead so rapidly within the last few years. They have progressed from the idea of a simple *political reform* to the idea of a *Social Revolution*.

The influence of the continental refugees, especially Marx, on the Harney group is obvious, and it was MacFarlane who produced the first English translation of the Communist Manifesto for Harney to publish in the *Red Republican*. But if Harney was prepared to dally with Marxian socialism, he was also open to the blandishments of Owenites and even Christian Socialists. Jones was not, and, although Harney's move was popular with the moderate Owenite wing of radicalism which he had previously attacked, it smacked too much of class compromise for Jones. Harney and Jones were two strong personalities, and they finally quarrelled in the spring of 1852. Jones started a new paper, the *People's Paper*, in May, while Harney moved towards the non-Socialist radicals such as Linton and the world of Joseph Cowen's personal brand of middle-class extremism in Newcastle upon Tyne (**53, 56**).

Much of later Chartism therefore came to centre on Jones. In his various publications, especially his *Notes to the People* (1851–52), Jones emerged as the leading strategist and ideologist of the working-class movement [**doc. 38**]. He tried to narrow the aims of popular radicalism until they were focused entirely on the acquisition of political power by the working classes through the Chartist organisation. Like O'Connor earlier, he saw temperance, co-operative associations, middle-class radicalism and the like as so many distractions, not harmful in themselves but damaging to Chartism as a movement to secure political power on a class base. Needless to say, his views endeared him to Marx and Engels who, especially after Harney's failure, regarded him as their most promising pupil in Britain. But Jones was more than this. Though Chartism now lacked the mass following of earlier years, he was still able to retain great popular appeal and affection. Jones, like Owen and Oastler, had clearly sacrificed himself for the people, and they responded with warmth. He had been born into the upper classes; his literary and legal talents were above average. His contemporaries were unaware that his moves towards radicalism had been precipitated by bankruptcy; all they saw was the genuineness of his conversion to the cause of the people in 1846, and the reality of the great sacrifices which this entailed. He ruined life and health in the cause. While he was in prison his wife and children were maintained by the Chartists of Halifax, where he had stood in the general election of 1847, securing 280 votes. He stood again in 1852, and got only thirty-eight votes (**63g**). Nevertheless, he continued to work for the reorganisation of Chartism, despite apathy from the rank and file and opposition from other Chartist leaders. More than anyone he can be said to have inherited the riches of O'Connor's ragged kingdom. He called a convention in Manchester in May 1852 to rally the remnants, but this and other similar efforts produced no lasting results. Finally, in 1858, he bowed to the inevitable when in February he called a conference to promote co-operation (but not compromise) with the middle classes (**56**). This resulted in the formation of the Political Reform Union, which should, however, be seen not as the end of Chartism but as the beginning of a new reform movement leading up to the Reform Act of 1867. Chartism by 1858 had long been dead.

The third prominent leader who survived into the 1850s still active in the cause was Bronterre O'Brien, whose National Reform League (founded 1849) was scarcely national but existed as a nucleus of extremist disciples in London. Dedicated to the ultra-radical views first expressed by O'Brien in the *Poor Man's Guardian* of the early 1830s, the O'Brienites (chief among whom were the brothers Charles and James Murray) did not need Marx to tell them about the class struggle. In themselves they represented an important native strand in English socialist thinking, linking the 1840s with the 1880s. O'Brien's distinctive views on currency reform and land nationalisation were maintained among them as they continued to meet at their headquarters in the Eclectic Institute, Denmark Street, Soho even after O'Brien's death in 1864, and they were to play an important part in the First International, which also met in the Eclectic Hall (**99**).

By this time, though, Chartism was no more than a memory. The fact that Gammage could write its history in 1854 is an indication that the movement was then already a thing of the past. There were still Chartists to process through the streets of London in 1856 to welcome a reprieved John Frost back from exile, but two years later, when Lord John Russell had awakened the reform issue with a new Reform Bill in Parliament, only 5,408 signatures could be collected in its support and only 17,684 in favour of the ballot (compared with 405,342 against the Sunday liquor traffic). The Crimean War (1854–56), with its revival of Urquhartism and diversion of public attention to foreign affairs, can best be regarded as the watershed between the early-Victorian era of Chartism and the mid-Victorian era of popular Liberalism.

Part Three: Perspectives

6 Strategy

Chartism was an extra-parliamentary pressure group operating outside the traditional political world. The question of how it was going to make its impact on that world was therefore of paramount importance. Behind the quarrels between the various leaders invariably lay disputes about strategy. Was Chartism to influence the parliamentary world through peaceful persuasion, or by acts of violence? Was it to maintain itself in independence, or sully its purity by co-operating with radicals of other classes whose aims were not always the same?

The contemporary Chartist historian, R. G. Gammage, employed the categories 'moral force' and 'physical force' to denote the two camps into which he saw Chartism dividing as early as 1839 (**7**). Since then historians have discounted too black-and-white a picture of rival camps, and have instead indicated the varying shades of grey into which Chartist opinions may more accurately be divided, but as a means of analysis Gammage's crude division remains appropriate (**39**). The belief of the artisans who started the Chartist movement in London was that the vote was a right, but that this right would most likely be conceded to working men who had proved themselves ready and able to exercise it in a responsible manner. Hence the insistence of this group on education, temperance, and moderation, and their anger at those leaders like O'Connor whose actions appeared to negate all they stood for. The Birmingham Political Union radicals shared the outlook of Lovett and his friends. They believed in the supremacy of reason and the triumph of the rational over the irrational. All working men had to do was to assert their rights, and Lovett's National Association plan assumed that the means to success lay in the conversion of public opinion. There is some justification for these views. The BPU had apparently succeeded in 1832 by mobilising public opinion, though not entirely without resort to threatening language, and in the longer term the extension of the franchise in 1867 to the urban artisans was to owe a great deal to their thrift, sobriety and level-headedness, which did so much to win Mr Gladstone over to their side (**24**).

In the short term, however, the moral force argument now appears singularly naive, for it failed to appreciate the nature of the parliamentary world and the real reason for the middle-class success in 1832. For, although the 'people', as the source of labour and producers of wealth, were at least as much an economic fact in the life of the country as were the middle-class manufacturers of 1832, the ruling class in Parliament did not see the matter in this light. The manufacturers were held to represent the whole manufacturing interest, and sufficient of them already had the vote to persuade the existing country interest of the need for reform. Moreover, a party within Parliament had become convinced of the need for reform. But throughout this time 'class' itself was never recognised as an 'interest' to be enfranchised; and the theory of political action still presumed a vertically rather than horizontally structured society. Except for a handful of radicals, few people in the parliamentary classes yet accepted the idea of the vote as a 'right'. The Chartists did not, therefore, simply represent the logical extension of a political theory accepted in 1832: they represented a new world which the old was not yet ready to receive.

The alternative strategy involved a resort to force to compel the parliamentary classes to yield. Again, the experience of the BPU and the demonstrations of May 1832 were held to be relevant, for then the government appeared to have conceded reform in response to the threat of force. Furthermore, the appeal to violence had to some extent been vindicated by the Anti-Poor Law movement in the North of England where riots, as in Huddersfield, had successfully prevented the election of a Board of Guardians clerk and so delayed by over a year the implementation of the Poor Law Amendment Act (**31**). Even the leaders of the Anti-Corn Law League were contemplating the use of violence to further their cause in 1842, though they wisely drew back, on the grounds that such force would not be widely enough supported (**34**). Against some people the threat of violence certainly worked. Middle-class radicals like Joseph Sturge were inclined to support universal suffrage as an alternative to revolution, but the forces of order were too strong for governments to need to take this line. Where the Chartists did resort to violence, as at Newport in 1839 or Bradford in 1848, it did little to further their cause. Far from panicking the middle classes into conceding Chartist demands, it fortified the alliance of property with order against them. The government was too powerful, having at its disposal the army, the London police, and, after the 1839 Rural Police Act, the beginnings of a force in the country. In the early 1840s the electric telegraph system was established, giving the government much better knowledge of what was going on in the country and facilitating the most effective deployment of police and troops, while the establishment of the railway network permitted the quick movement of forces to trouble-spots (**86**) [**doc. 9**]. In 1848 the electric telegraph was the eyes and ears of the ministers as they took complete control of the situation (**65f**). A concerted rising in 1839, before these technical developments, would have stood the best chance of success, though the very lack of national communications proved to be a handicap to the Chartists as well [**doc. 12**]. The Northern commander, Sir Charles Napier, did not underestimate the Chartists, but the emotion he felt for them was not fear but pity [**doc. 13**].

The debate between moral and physical force strategies occupied much time at the 1839 Convention, for the delegates had to face the possibility that the House of Commons might not be impressed by 1,200,000 signatures [**doc. 4**]. Was the Convention meant to rival Parliament or simply to petition Parliament? The language of the Convention was heated, causing moderates like Dr Wade to resign, and the resolutions in favour of resistance to injustice and oppression, put forward by Harney and the London Democratic Association, received only six votes, including that of John Frost. The clearest tactical leadership came from Bronterre O'Brien, who argued that only a concerted action of the whole people could be successful. He was clearly right. A general strike *would* serve to remind Members of Parliament of the economic power of the unenfranchised; a fully national rising *would* stretch the forces of law and order beyond breaking point, as Napier was well aware. But the country was ready for neither, and talk of physical force, aided by the activities of government spies, would simply provoke premature local risings [**doc. 6**]. This was O'Brien's position in 1839 and it became Harney's in 1842 and Jones's in 1848.

Could the Chartists ever have secured that unity of action which alone would have made physical force a real possibility? A general strike was hardly feasible at a time of depression, for the workers would starve before their masters [**doc. 20**], and the workforce was never sufficiently united to preclude the use of blackleg labour. The weakness of the strike weapon had been demonstrated in 1834, and in 1842 some employers may actually have been glad to have their works closed for a few weeks during the depression. Similarly, there is little evidence to suggest that a successful rising could have been organised, even in South Wales where the massed Chartists were out-thought and out-fought by thirty soldiers. Furthermore, it is important to ask whether many Chartists actually wanted a revolution.

The answer to this question might seem obvious, for the many speeches on the subject appear to suggest that the leaders were seriously considering violent action. Yet the age of the Chartists was also the age of melodrama on the stage, and fire and brimstone in the pulpit (**107**). Violence was part of the language of the period, and should not necessarily be taken at its surface valuation. J. R. Stephens and Richard Oastler were denouncing sin very much in the language of Old Testament prophecy. O'Connor's oratory too had many of the same characteristics, though it was not so obviously biblical. 'Peaceably if we may, forcibly if we must' was his attitude, though he and other leaders often spoke as though they must. The Chartists were undoubtedly arming, avowedly for self-protection, and there was a great deal of anger born of misery in the villages of depressed workers like the handloom weavers, but the call to rise never came after 1839. When O'Connor capitulated at Kennington Common in 1848 he looked 'pale and frightened' [**doc. 35**]; doubtless he was haunted by the ghost of physical force which was his other self.

The truth was that neither he nor most of the other leaders had faced up to the problem of Chartist strategy. They simply hoped the problem would go away. Cries implying sedition were mixed up, almost at random, with signs of the utmost legality. When the Convention in 1839 discussed arming, the speakers in favour stressed the *legality* of bearing weapons in self defence, and, throughout the Chartist troubles, most of the leaders (and followers), for most of the time, tried to stay within the framework of the law, not simply to avoid arrest and imprisonment, but out of genuine respect for the law. When the rioters of 1842 seemed to threaten the peace they did so in the name of justice, peace, law and order [**doc. 22**]. This was as much a part of the Chartist rhetoric as resistance, God and death.

So one is forced to conclude that the real weakness of Chartist strategy is that they had no coherent or effective strategy to offer. The moral force educationalists were hopelessly naive about the preconditions for change, and the physical force advocates, caught up in their own rhetoric, were unable or unwilling to separate fact from fancy, and to ask whether the use of force was either possible or desirable. Those leaders who thought most clearly – O'Brien, Jones and, at times, Harney [**doc. 32**] – were also the most sanguine in their expectations. They saw that Chartism had to rest on the mass of the people, but that the people needed more organisation before they could act for change.

In the meantime, the second strategy, that of an alliance with the middle-class radicals, offered itself. Broadly speaking, moral force Chartists were most open to such co-operation, though eventually all the leaders came round to this point of view. The Chartists had no parliamentary party, and were not likely to get one until the Charter became the law of the land, so they had either to frighten, or to co-operate with, existing forces within the political nation, Tory, Whig or Radical. The factory reformers and Anti-Poor Law agitators had found some Tory support, but for political reform the choice was between the Whigs and the Radicals. The legend of the Whig Betrayal prevented much co-operation with the former, while the association of the O'Connellite and Manchester School radicals with the poor law and political economy prevented such a tactical alliance from prospering at first [**doc. 23**]. The defeats of 1839, 1842 and 1848 were needed to bring successive groups of Chartists round to the idea of a tactical alliance with other parties.

The Charter had, of course, been born of the alliance forged in London between Radical MPs and representatives of the working class, and the prominent part played by the BPU underlined the fact that early Chartism was not an exclusively working-class movement (**88**). Even in the darkest days, sympathisers were to be found among the higher classes, including T. S. Duncombe, the Chartists' best friend in Parliament, and Sir Charles Napier, commander of the troops in the North between 1839 and 1841. But the tone given to Chartism by the physical force men of the North precluded any genuine attempt at co-operation with the higher classes, and the *Northern Star* was openly contemptuous of such efforts (**38a**).

The fate of Joseph Sturge's Complete Suffrage Union illustrates both the difficulties of co-operation between the classes and the danger in generalising about Chartist attitudes, for the attempt at union had failed by the end of 1842, not only because of O'Connor's opposition, but also because of Lovett's (**57**). The artisan Chartist educationalists had no less a sense of working-class consciousness than the middle-class lawyers such as O'Connor, O'Brien and later Jones, who spoke in the name of the working classes. The pride, dignity and self-respect of the artisan, as much as the bitter mistrust felt by the textile operative, served to keep working men apart and to ensure that any alliance with a higher class would be hard won and for tactical purposes only. Despite the earlier moves, therefore, it was only after 1848 that a significant shift occurred in Chartist thinking about this tactic. Then, after twelve years principally spent denouncing the hypocrisy of the middle classes, the *Northern Star* could finally recognise what had become inevitable and agree to work alongside the middle-class radicals of the National Financial and Parliamentary Reform Association [**doc. 37**].

This strategy was to bring some success in the 1860s, but even had it been adopted earlier it would scarcely have brought success. The BPU had provided a false model for the 1830s, and the Anti-Corn Law League was equally misleading in the 1840s. The middle-class radicals were not all-powerful. The Anti-Corn Law League did, as a matter of fact, appeal to many operatives and had considerable backing from manufacturers, but its success lay in the attitude of Sir Robert Peel (**33**). If the Chartists and Leaguers had allied, and if this had not frightened most of the League's members away, then possibly a middle-class campaign with the threat of working-class pressure behind it *might* have persuaded Parliament to take the Charter seriously, but the hypothesis rests on too many highly dubious assumptions. Even with such an alliance after 1848, and even with both Lord John Russell and Benjamin Disraeli prepared to reopen the Reform issue in Parliament in the 1850s, any modification of the franchise had to wait twenty years and even so still be the product more of inter-party rivalry than of concession to external pressure.

The depressing conclusion appears to be that the Chartists in the 1840s had no hope of success. Rather than ask why they failed, one would do better to ask why they thought they could succeed and why they endured so long in the face of so many setbacks. Such questions would at least move the discussion of Chartism away from the search for a scapegoat. A frequent presumption, which lies at the heart of Gammage's interpretation, is that Chartism failed because of defective leadership, that defective leader being Feargus O'Connor. How valid is this interpretation?

7 Leadership

Leadership was central to the development of Chartism, if not to its failure, for its leaders determined the tone, policies and direction of the movement. Without Lovett, O'Brien, Harney, O'Connor and Jones – and many others – Chartism would have been a very different creature, if it had existed at all. The historian's assessment of the movement, and of their role in it, is especially difficult, for most of the sources were written by these people themselves who present the history of Chartism as seen through their own eyes [**docs 18, 19**]. The one exception, Gammage's history, is the work of a minor Chartist, but he had strong preferences for certain leaders, notably Lovett and O'Brien, and strong antipathies to others, especially O'Connor, so that too great a reliance on his extremely personal view has led to many distortions (**7**). Of the autobiographies, the best-known are by Lovett and Thomas Cooper (**42, 43**), though others do exist and are now being made more readily available (**47**). The periodicals and newspapers are almost entirely concerned with the writings or reports of the speeches of the leaders, though one can gather insights into the followers through the local reports and the correspondence columns. Official records in the Home Office files contain their own bias, but at least they yield some information about less prominent Chartists (thought still prominent enough to be noticed by the authorities) (**4, 86b**) [**doc. 14**]. The historian has always to be aware that the sources available to him are inclined to give a picture of Chartism from the top, and that this might be a misleading picture. Nevertheless the leaders were right to attribute importance to their own efforts, for Chartism was an *organised* movement for political change, not a *spontaneous* rising of the people.

The backgrounds of the national leaders vary a good deal. Many, like Hetherington (b.1792), Watson (b.1799) and Vincent (b.1813), printers, Lovett (b.1800), cabinet-maker, and Thomas Cooper (b.1805), shoemaker, were artisans in origin. Others, such as Harney (b.1817), a cabin-boy turned London pot-boy and

favoured relevation in the
early years.

vendor of the unstamped, were not even that; none of them had had more than an elementary education. On the other hand, O'Brien (b.1804), O'Connor (b.1796) and Jones (b.1819) had all had a legal training (**48, 50, 58**). If one discounts O'Connor's claim to be descended from the Kings of Ireland, Jones was the most high-born, the son of a cavalry officer who was equerry to Ernest, Duke of Cumberland, later King of Hanover, after whom Jones was named (**56**). Their ages vary, but, except for Harney and Jones, they were all men of mature years when Chartism commenced. The founders of the movement were a close-knit group. Of the six who signed the preamble to the Charter – Lovett, Hetherington, Watson, Cleave, Moore and Vincent – the first four were old friends and allies from the early 1830s, Moore married Watson's niece, and Vincent married Cleave's daughter. O'Brien and Harney also had worked for Hetherington in the war of the unstamped. This group constituted what might be called a professional leadership which, by its very professionalism, was in danger of becoming detached from the movement it led.

Some degree of detachment, though, was a necessary characteristic of leadership, and this was the essence of O'Connor's appeal. His was the most important and significant leadership because he was able to combine elements of camaraderie and detachment, democracy and paternalism. He was both part of the movement and above it, as his regular addresses in the *Northern Star* 'To the Fustian Jackets, the Blistered Hands, and Unshorn Chins' of his supporters illustrate by their familiar and yet slightly condescending tone. The picture given of O'Connor's leadership by Gammage, most recently echoed in the study of Chartism by J. T. Ward, is unfavourable. In their view O'Connor was the man who took Chartism out of the hands of the thoughtful and moderate Lovett, and transformed it into the victim of his own megalomania (**7, 37**). The talents of Lovett, O'Brien and, eventually, Harney were scorned by a man who could and would brook no opposition, but who led the Chartists on to self-destruction by his braggadocio, his conceit and his inconsistency. The case is a powerful one. Yet there is also a more sympathetic view, for O'Connor has been very much the victim of a history written by other leaders, who were in no position to be impartial witnesses [**docs 30, 31**]. It is true that O'Connor transformed Lovett's and Attwood's Chartism out of recognition, but this stands condemned only if one accepts that the strategy adopted by Lovett and Attwood would have succeeded. O'Connor's advent can be seen as saving them from the recognition of the sterility of their own approach, and as supplying them with a convenient scapegoat. Similarly Oastlerites might despair of the way in which O'Connor took over the factory and Anti-Poor Law agitations, but these were stagnating anyway. Their transformation into Chartism rescued them from defeat, as much as it did the London artisans and men of Birmingham. What O'Connor did do was to link the various aspects of Chartism, and whilst dividing the leadership he united the movement. Despite the preliminary successes of the LWMA and BPU missionaries, it was O'Connor who succeeded in transforming a pressure group into a truly national movement. He built on the work of others, and with the NCA and the *Northern Star* he was to continue to do so, but he was no mere plagiarist. The sum of Chartism was greater than its parts, and that extra ingredient was O'Connor's personal magic. Thomas Cooper, who began as an O'Connorite but later turned against him, recalled Feargus in his prime:

> There was much that was attractive in him when I first knew him. His fine manly form and his powerful baritone voice gave him great advantages as a popular leader. His conversation was rich in Irish humour and often evinced a shrewd knowledge of character (**43**) [**doc. 32**].

Cooper also perceived O'Connor's real strength, that of the popular demagogue.

> For the demagogue, or popular 'leader', is rather the people's instrument than their director. He keeps the lead and is the people's mouthpiece, hand and arm, either for good or evil, because his quick sympathies are with the people; while his temperament, nature and energetic will fit him for the very post which the people's voice assigns him.

In this view, to call O'Connor a demagogue (usually seen as a term of abuse) is to praise him. Men like Lovett, who would be for ever *improving* the working classes, were not typical of those classes, and it can be no surprise that Lovett failed to win the enduring sympathy of more than a tiny proportion of the people. O'Connor lived closer to their hearts. His strange mixture of contradictions – at times radical and Tory, progressive and reactionary, democrat and paternalist – accurately reflected the contradictions inherent in the working classes as a whole. As G. J. Holyoake recalled, without malice, 'Logic was not his strong point, and he had colossal incoherence' (**108**).

This is not to say that O'Connor was not also a leader. His insistence on the Charter and no distractions was as single-minded and sensible a policy as Cobden's similar insistence that the Anti-Corn Law League should take up no other issues, however congenial they might be (**34**). His Land Plan might be seen as one such distraction, yet without it O'Connor might not have been able to hold Chartism together at all in the mid 1840s. The scheme may have been ill-thought-out and illegal, but it attracted many more supporters than did Robert Owen's grand community schemes. It did not create the hope of a return to the land, but responded to a hope already deeply embedded in the consciousness of many working people. Feargus O'Connor was fed by, and then led, the popular mood. Finally, no less than any other leader, he was a martyr to the cause. His enemies said he profited by the movement, especially by the *Northern Star*, but those profits and tenfold more energy were given back to the movement. Like others he went to prison for his leadership, and his health suffered in the process. Cynics might say that the Land Plan was the product of madness; it is more likely that his excessive brandy drinking and final breakdown were the consequence of the disastrous chaos of the Land Plan, and not its cause (**38a, 54a**).

One opponent of O'Connor, writing in 1871, commented (still with some bitterness), 'What Chartism might have been and achieved if O'Connor had not pulled it down into the gutter it would be useless to speculate' (**109**). The assumption was that Chartism would have been the better for O'Connor's absence [**doc. 42**], but this is neither an easy nor an obvious assumption to make. Who else could have combined the merits, as well as the admitted faults, of a Stephens, an Oastler, a Hunt, a Cobbett, a Lovett and a Hetherington, as orator, prophet, romantic, organiser and journalist? The matter *is* worth speculating upon.

One leader who does emerge with honour from Gammage's history is Bronterre O'Brien, a man whose powers of oratory were different from but comparable to those of O'Connor, an experienced journalist with a radical reputation going back to the days when he had edited the *Poor Man's Guardian*, and before the advent of Ernest Jones the most advanced theorist of the Chartist movement, dubbed by O'Connor 'the schoolmaster of Chartism'. Unlike O'Connor, he was a clearsighted and consistent strategist, opposed to premature action at the 1839 Convention, and yet essentially of the physical force party. Until he parted company with O'Connor, over the latter's support of Tory candidates at the 1841 general election, he was one of the best writers on the *Northern Star*, and his views earned a widespread respect. But after 1841 he became increasingly isolated. Opposed to O'Connor and yet not reconciled to the Lovett faction, he was left high and dry without a significant following in the movement. He gathered round him his disciples and continued to be admired for his intellectual powers, but in Gammage's own praise of O'Brien it is significant that he felt obliged to explain *why* O'Brien should be accounted a good orator, for plainly some contemporaries were misguided enough to think that he was not (**7**). He was steeped in the romanticism of the French Revolution and was one of the first to see the importance of Robespierre as a heroic figure, but the model was inapplicable to England. Had there been an English revolution, O'Brien might have been its Robespierre (or its Lenin), but this was not to be. On emerging from gaol in 1841 he was, in G. D. H. Cole's words, 'a deeply disappointed and disillusioned man'. His resignation from the Convention in 1848 was the last symbol of his detachment from the cause (**38a, 48, 55**).

The claims of G. J. Harney might also be considered, though he belonged to the younger generation of radicals and was only fifteen at the time of the Reform Act, when he first entered Hetherington's employment and met O'Brien. From O'Brien he learned to love the tradition of the French Revolution – he saw himself as Marat to O'Brien's Robespierre – and to think of the growing radical struggle in terms of class. He made his mark as a leader of London extremism in the later 1830s, still very much influenced by O'Brien though moving closer to O'Connor. Though increasingly convinced after 1839 that the time was not yet ripe for physical force, he became an O'Connorite in the 1840s, and sub-editor and then editor of the *Northern Star*. Not till 1850 did the two men part company, so for much of the Chartist period he is to be placed firmly in O'Connor's camp. Could he have succeeded where the master failed? Gammage's picture is distorted by the connection with O'Connor, but it does not seem wholly unfair, and Harney himself confirms it [**doc. 32**]. He was no orator: he was an honest enthusiast with some journalistic talent. His breadth of vision, drawing in the European scene of revolutionary activity, was not an immediately popular one, while his differences with Marx and Engels in the early 1850s barred him from that particular tradition just as he was beginning to add experience to youthful idealism (**48, 53**).

Ernest Jones was the only other Chartist leader of Harney's age, being born in 1819, though unlike Harney he did not enter the English radical movement until 1846. Thereafter he did display both the intellect of O'Brien and the popularity of O'Connor, and in the 1850s gathered up much of O'Connor's former support. He might, had he been older and available, have made Chartism a different movement ten years earlier, but that is a supposition too hypothetical to make. Had he lived through 1839–42 he might equally, like O'Brien, have become detached from the mainstream of the movement (**48, 56**).

The fact remains that, though O'Connor did drive out of Chartism all obvious rivals, yet none of them could really have replaced him. And to expect government by committee, which seems to have been the LWMA ideal, was totally unrealistic. The earlier radical movement had been bitterly divided between Cobbett and Hunt; division was so much a condition of early working-class radicalism that to expect anything different would be utopian. Chartism therefore merges with O'Connorism despite the many protests against the trend, and Chartism was destined to be led by 'unquestionably the best-loved, as well as the most-hated, man in the Chartist movement' (**48**).

8 Localities

Chartism was diverse not only in its leadership but in its local history, indeed so much so that Chartism might seem in danger of disintegrating entirely as a national concept. Seen overall there is a fragmented unity and continuity; seen from close quarters the fragments loom larger and that unity and continuity are much less obvious. In his pioneer collection of local Chartist studies, Asa Briggs rightly reminded all students that 'a study of Chartism must begin with a proper appreciation of regional and local diversity' (**62**). Briggs's collection was a starting point, since when other historians – amateur and professional, teachers and students – have been filling in more and more of the gaps. What follows can only be a partial and inadequate survey, drawing largely on studies less readily available than those in the Briggs collection.

The British Isles may be divided into several types of locality: agricultural areas; those with declining industries; those with new industries; large towns, small towns, industrial villages; areas based on extractive industries such as coal-mining; areas of textile manufacture, or iron and heavy engineering industry; Wales, Scotland and Ireland, each with its own distinctive characteristics; and London, always in all matters a special case. The distribution of Chartist activities suggests that the central valley of Scotland and the east coast lowlands accounted for most Scottish Chartism, with the Glasgow area predominating, while in England the textile areas of Lancashire and Yorkshire were overwhelmingly important, with other centres in the North-east, the Midlands, and London. Most reports of activities relate to the period between 1838 and 1842, after which Chartism in many areas died out or was reduced to a shadow of its former self.

London is a problem for the historian. As the largest centre of population and concentration of trades, as well as the seat of government and home of most of the national leaders, it ought to have been at the centre of affairs, as it had been in the 1790s. Yet delegates from the provinces who attended the 1839 Convention were disappointed at the lukewarm atmosphere of London [**doc. 8**]. Nor was this peculiar to Chartism. J. B. Smith of the Anti-Corn Law League described London in 1839 as 'something like descending into an ice box' (**21**). No really satisfactory explanation of this has been offered, yet the fact is crucial to the development of radical politics in England in the nineteenth century, as compared with those of France, where the capital city dominated the whole country and fostered its revolutions.

The structure of its industry was offered as an explanation of London's weakness by Francis Place, and he was experienced enough to have a worthwhile view. Apart from the building trades and brewing industry, much of London's employment was in small units, geographically dispersed in workshops. There were over four hundred different trades, requiring different skills and offering different levels of remuneration. With the exception of the Spitalfields weavers, there was no group comparable to the depressed outworkers of the textile areas of the provinces. This is not to claim that London was exempt from poverty – the reverse would be true – but the level of employment in London was not subject to violent fluctuations, as in the North. Not all trades prospered, but neither were all depressed at once. Whereas a collapse in employment in a factory town would deplete consumer power locally, with an immediate effect on tradesmen and shopkeepers, such a general impact was rare in the broadly based economy of London, though Prince Albert in 1848 was to deplore the cutback in public spending for its effect on employment in London and hence on Chartist unrest (**65–65f, 110**).

Size has also been blamed for the weakness of London radicalism. In the 1790s, when London had given the lead, the population had still been under one million. By 1841 it had more than doubled to two million. The 'Great Wen', as Cobbett called it, was in reality too big to act as a unity: divided into different areas by local government and geography, it was in reality several towns, not just one; Marylebone, for example, was separately represented at the 1839 Convention.

Sectionalism, of an economic or geographical nature, was made worse by the divisions within the national leadership, and for the metropolis to be the natural centre of operations could be more of a hindrance than a help. Early London Chartism was divided between Lovett and Harney, and later between Lovett and O'Connor, while the divisions between O'Connor and O'Connell lost the considerable Irish population of the capital to the Chartists until 1847–48. Because the LWMA did not think of itself as leading a mass movement, the Convention of 1839 was to find London ill-prepared. The capital city had contributed only 19,000 signatures to the National Petition by May 1839, compared with 100,000 from the West Riding.

This last evidence seems incontrovertible, but the explanations are not entirely convincing. Small workshops were a notorious breeding ground for radicalism; men in tailoring or shoemaking could discuss ideas at work, to keep their minds occupied, in a way not open to operatives in a noisy factory, and the distances involved in passing from Battersea to Bethnal Green were less than those in passing from Huddersfield to Bradford, yet the West Riding was able to act cohesively, its separate and distinct components reinforcing one another. But undoubtedly the broadly based economy of London and the lack of unusual distress remain relevant. Single-industry towns which prospered in the 1840s, like Glossop and Swindon, however unlike London in other respects, similarly showed that Chartism without adequate roots in economic deprivation was likely to be a sickly plant.

The success of Chartism in the diverse local communities of the textile areas, and the past history of London, however, suggest that the explanations are inadequate in part because they are redundant; for, although Chartism in London was weak in 1839, by 1841–42 it had grown much stronger there, but not at the level usually surveyed by historians. The history of the London working class is to be sought in its trade societies and in the world of taverns, clubs and friendly societies. Just as F. C. Mather has found the real connection between trade unions and Chartism at this level in the Manchester area in 1842 (**78**), so historians have located it in London, where Chartism grew not out of ready-made mass movements for factory reform or the abolition of the Poor Law Amendment Act, but out of the richness of artisan club life (**65, 65d**). The peak of London local organisations is to be found not in 1839, when there were no more than twenty-two, but in 1842, when there were as many as thirty-eight. In 1844 Chartism could still boast in London more local activity than it could in 1839, and when in 1845 O'Connor wished to broaden the appeal of the *Northern Star* as a Chartist and trade union newspaper, he moved it from Leeds to London. The NCA similarly became very much a London organisation with a majority of London members on the Executive.

The problem was how to unite these small pockets of local Chartism in London. In the early 1830s the Grand National Consolidated Trades Union had attempted to bring the various trades together, with only moderate success, but the 1834 Copenhagen Fields demonstration in support of the Tolpuddle martyrs showed what the combined forces of the London trades could achieve. Not all this manpower was to be attracted to Chartism, but there was much more Chartism among the richness of metropolitan journeyman life than a history of the LWMA might suggest. The NCA was successful in London, where O'Connor became the favourite national leader and where his Land Plan attracted much interest. By 1842, there were at least sixteen Chartist localities attached to specific trades, chiefly shoemakers and tailors, and the metropolitan delegates to the Convention were holding weekly meetings. So by 1848, with the accession of Irish support, London was capable of presenting more energy and conveying more of a threat to the government than it had in 1839. As in Leeds, this activity also expressed itself in local government at the level of vestry and parish politics. In Finsbury, Marylebone, Lambeth and St Pancras local activists involved themselves in the democratic open vestries, where the franchise belonged to all ratepayers and voting was by ballot.

Even so, if any one region has to be selected as having stamped its peculiar nature on Chartism as a whole, that would have to be not London but the textile areas of Lancashire, Cheshire and the West Riding of Yorkshire. Here there were great differences between towns, according to the nature of the prevailing industry, but all were united in a common historical experience, especially in the factory and poor law struggles (**38a**). The cotton industry of Lancashire and the worsted industry of Bradford and Halifax were the most highly developed, throwing up militancy among depressed workers such as handloom weavers and woolcombers. These changes were only just beginning to affect the woollen trade, though early mills like Gott's in Leeds had pointed the way, and the threat was as good as the fact. Manchester, and to a lesser extent Leeds, displayed some of the 'metropolitan' characteristics noted in London, with their broader social and economic basis which fostered comparative moderation, while the smaller, single industry towns and depressed industrial villages around them furnished more extreme varieties of Chartism. In Ashton, Stalybridge, Stockport, Oldham and Bolton we find the strongholds of industrial Chartism in Lancashire, and in Yorkshire Halifax, Bradford and Barnsley were noted centres. This contrast between the provincial centre and its dependent communities also applies to the

West Midlands, with Birmingham more moderate than the Black Country, where the depressed outworkers in the metal industries present a contrast to the usually better-paid artisans of Birmingham itself, though the distinction between the two was always likely to be less in times of unemployment and slack trade (**62, 63**).

In contrast to the basic industrial areas of England we might compare two ports, Newcastle and Bristol, both of which have found their local historians of Chartism. The story of Bristol makes dismal reading. The record of the city in the Reform Bill agitation might have suggested that it was to be a centre of Chartist activity, especially of the more violent kind. By August 1837 it had a Working Men's Association, the area was being roused by Henry Vincent, and mass meetings were held on Brandon Hill. But John Cannon's opinion is that the local Chartists were already flagging by the time of Vincent's arrest in 1839 (**66**). Following his subsequent adoption of moderation and the complete suffrage platform, the Bristol Chartists never recovered their violent outlook, and, apart from a brief revival in the summer of 1848, they were no more than 'a small and insignificant clique'. Indeed, Bristol was to prove throughout the Chartist period a far less violent centre than Bath, which with a fifth of the population had 1,800 Chartists compared with Bristol's 800. Bath, Trowbridge and Bradford-on-Avon, which were centres of depressed woollen manufacture, held out far better prospects for the Chartists than did Bristol, which, in Cannon's word, was 'tepid' (**62e, 66**).

The story of Tyneside has some similarities. With a Working Men's Association founded by Tommy Hepburn, the former miners' leader, in 1837, Newcastle became a centre of early 'physical force' Chartism, and the political base of G. J. Harney and Dr John Taylor, two of the most outspoken delegates at the 1839 Convention. But with the exception of the Winlaton ironworkers, depressed by competition from newer ironworks and with time on their hands to manufacture pikes, there was little basis for a prolonged and deeply rooted local Chartist movement. O'Connor was a popular figure, but much of the actual response in the 1840s was organised from outside. The local leader, Robert Lowery of South Shields, like Vincent, moved rapidly from extremism to moderation after 1840, while another local extremist, Thomas Devyr, was lost when he emigrated to America in 1840. What support there was in the early years came more from the outlying colliery villages of recent settlement, such as Seghill, where a settled conservative community had not had time to form, and from the smaller towns and villages down river from Newcastle. The heady days of mass meetings and widespread support had largely gone by late 1840, and after 1842 mining trade unionism attracted attention away from the radicals. Nevertheless Chartism in the North-east had stronger roots than this might imply, for the Land Plan stimulated a revival of interest which put the men of Tyneside among the foremost contributors to the scheme (**68**). The position of Chartism in the Newcastle area must therefore stand somewhere between that of the Manchester area on the one hand and Bristol on the other.

In this way the national history of Chartism, though generally reflected in the localities, is never entirely repeated there. The coal-mining areas of the North-east might be compared with those of South Wales, and the depressed linen weavers of Stokesley or Barnsley with those of Newtown and Llanidloes in Wales, but with additional ingredients peculiar to the Principality – Welsh culture and history, the sense of alienation from English capitalists, English landlords and an Anglican Church. Wales also had its own traditions of violent protest – the 'Scotch cattle' terrorism of the Valleys, and the 'Rebecca riots' of the countryside which broke out in 1839 and 1842–43 (**62f, 73, 73a**).

Scotland likewise should be regarded as more than a mere appendage of England, with its different legal, educational and religious institutions, as well as differences in economic development. The handloom weavers of the West were stronger than their fellows in Lancashire in a cotton industry not yet given over to the power loom, while a rapid expansion in the metallurgical industries (output of pig-iron increasing threefold between 1835 and 1839, and again between 1839 and 1853) kept the economy buoyant. Between 1836 and 1840 fifty-three steamships were launched on the Clyde, the Govan Yard was laid down in 1840, and the economic basis of much of hunger politics was undermined. But not entirely, for the delay in the introduction of power looms was partly because handloom weavers' wages were low and Irish cheap labour was readily available (**72**). The depressions of 1841 and 1842 hit the Scots like everyone else. Scotland was a very early centre of Chartist activity, and had its violent moments as a section of radicals and trade unions warmed to O'Connor's speeches on behalf of the five convicted leaders of the striking cotton spinners in 1837, but Scotland had not had the Poor Law Amendment Act of 1834. Moderate reformism and moral force were the prevailing tones of Scottish Chartism, where Arthur O'Neil's Christian Chartism thrived [**doc. 26**]. Though O'Connor remained popular, Glasgow also threw up the eccentric James Moir, who was elected to the City Council in 1848, and 'Parson' James Adams, who was the Chartist preacher at the Nelson Street Chapel (**62g, 72a**).

All-pervasive, but most distinct of all, was the Irish connection. In Ireland itself Chartism was not widely established. The opposition of Daniel O'Connell and the identification of Chartism with England long prevented O'Brien's and O'Connor's dream of a united movement against the English ruling class. O'Connellites broke up a Dublin meeting attended by Robert Lowery in 1839, just as they were to break up Chartist meetings in England [**doc. 18**], and not till 1841 did Chartism make much headway at all. In August of that year, the Irish Universal Suffrage Association was formed, linking small Chartist discussion groups in Dublin, Belfast and several other Irish towns, but regular meetings were discontinued in 1844 and there was only a short revival in 1848 (**74**). Nevertheless the Irish in England contributed an important element to Chartism at all levels, from O'Connor and O'Brien to local men like Thomas Ainge Devyr of Tyneside and George White of the West Riding. James Campbell, first secretary of the NCA, was Irish, as were Thomas Clarke and Christopher Doyle, both leading members of the Executive. Irish names occur among the rank and file, as among the linen weavers of Barnsley and in the list of those tried at Lancaster in 1843. Finally, in 1848, with the temporary realisation of O'Connor's dream, the Irish played a major part in the last days of Chartism, especially its more violent aspects. The Irish, with their tradition of hostility to British rule, brought with them to England both grievances and experience which had an important effect on the English movement (**38a, 74a**).

So, in all the richness of its local and regional characteristics, the Chartist movement ebbed and flowed from the late 1830s to the early 1850s. The localities helped determine the national rhythms and were in turn determined by them. Necessary though this study of local movements is, though, there is a danger that an exclusive concern with local history, no less than the older historical emphasis on the quarrels between the leaders, will distort the overall picture, and conceal the very real unity which lay at the heart of diversity.

9 National Communications

Chartism, like other popular movements, was held together in three ways: by its leaders touring the country, addressing mass rallies in the manner of Henry Hunt; by its formal structure of organisation, especially the National Charter Association; and through its press.

Despite their wide differences of opinion, the role of the national leaders should not be underestimated, particularly at public meetings. These were a practical demonstration of the great fact of Chartism's existence as a movement. Vast meetings in the open air drew together local forces from a whole region as a symbolic expression of class solidarity [**doc. 2**]. The leaders could breathe in this spirit and carry it from region to region. But this alone was not enough. The leader saw an untypical view of his movement from the platform, and O'Connor might be forgiven for sometimes having an inflated image of his following. Also, not even O'Connor could be in more than one place at once. With short bursts of activity, as in 1838–39 or 1841–42, the national leaders, supplemented by local speakers, could hope to rouse widespread enthusiasm, but the meeting was not in itself sufficient to sustain this. Moreover, someone had to arrange the meetings in the first place.

So, even in the days of apparently spontaneous Chartism in 1838 and 1839, the role of local Working Men's Associations, founded by missionaries from London, Birmingham or Glasgow, was of crucial importance [**doc. 3**]. After the imprisonment of national and local leaders in 1839–40, the decision to give Chartism an overall permanent organisation in the NCA was therefore both natural and sensible. It was not, of course, the only such body. Scotland had its own Central Committee, and London its National Association, but the NCA was the most long-lasting and widely-accepted of all the Chartist organisations. It was founded in Manchester in July 1840, but thereafter extended itself throughout the industrial districts of England, then more widely across the country, into Wales and Scotland, with a permanent Executive sitting in London. Under its auspices lecturing circuits were arranged among the localities, and a general framework established which enabled Chartism to survive as a movement between 1842 and 1848. Through it O'Connor launched his Land Plan, the arrangements for regular Conventions were made, and the second and third petitions organised. Though it never became an exclusively O'Connorite body, it was closely associated with him. At its height it claimed about 50,000 members, falling to about 2,000 after 1842, and it represented the hardcore of Chartist support throughout its existence (**38**).

National organisation was also promoted in the 1840s by developments in communications, though these helped the government as well. In 1839 there was no railway network, and even in 1842, when Thomas Cooper wished to travel from the Potteries to Manchester, he walked to Macclesfield to catch a coach (**43**). The lecturer bound from England for West Scotland had to take a boat from Liverpool to Glasgow. Unlike the Anti-Corn Law League and the Owenites, the Chartists do not appear to have deliberately exploited the potential of the Penny Post, but the general quickening of communications must have greatly helped their lecturers and the collection and distribution of news and propaganda. Once England, Wales and Scotland had been brought within the same speedy communications network, a national movement was much easier to maintain.

Central to this national propaganda was the Chartist press. The pioneer of the radical newspaper had been William Cobbett, whose *Weekly Political Register* helped shape the direction of many radical careers in the first third of the nineteenth century, and the press as a weapon had been sharpened by Hetherington in the war of the unstamped in the early 1830s. All this experience was gathered up in the Chartist press, and especially in the *Northern Star*, in the later 1830s and 1840s. Each Chartist group or leader, and many individual regions, had their own periodicals or newspapers, most of them short-lived. The followers of Lovett had the *Charter* (1839–40), and Harney's views were put forward in the London *Democrat* (1839). The North-east had the *Northern Liberator*, set up by A. H. Beaumont in 1837, which co-ordinated and stimulated activities in the area until December 1840; and the West Country had Vincent's *Western Vindicator* (1839–42). Most successful was the Scottish *Chartist Circular* (1839–42), edited by William Thompson, a former secretary of the handloom weavers' union. At its height in 1839 the *Circular* was selling 22,500 copies a week, overtaking the *Scottish Patriot* (1839–41) which became the official organ of the Universal Suffrage Central Committee for Scotland in 1840, and which O'Connor likened to his *Northern Star* (**62g**). In fact nothing could be quite like the *Northern Star*, for, though it was originally based on the West Riding, it was never just a local newspaper. It sold more copies, reached more people, travelled to more parts of the country, and lasted longer than any other Chartist paper. Its columns were the arteries through which the blood of Chartism flowed, bringing the whole body life (**96**).

The Northern Star and Leeds General Advertiser, to give the paper its full and significant title, was originally projected as a local paper by a group of radicals led by William Hill, a Swedenborgian preacher from Hull. But the energy which went into raising funds by popular subscription, and the early financial risks, were O'Connor's: it was his paper and, through him, the movement's. Hill was editor, and the first number, stamped and sold at 4½d, was published in Leeds by Joshua Hobson on 18 November 1837. Its voice was, as Hobson's *Voice of the West Riding* had been, aggressively radical. It spoke the anger of the Anti-Poor Law movement, the frustration of the Ten Hours movement, the class-consciousness of the unstamped, and the hope of the radical reformers. In short, it established, even before the publication of the Charter, that movement which was to become Chartism, O'Connor's Chartism.

The strength of the paper, and its importance in Chartism, was its ability to act as a two-way channel of communication in similar manner to the rebellious unstamped. Though O'Connor gave his editors a relatively free hand, it was for him no less of a personal organ than Cobbett's *Weekly Political Register* had been for his great predecessor. The *Star* spoke to its readers as a personal friend, now flattering, now rebuking, but always in a spirit of comradeship [**docs 31, 32**]. One Newcastle radical later recalled how he, as a boy, had had to read the *Northern Star* to his illiterate parents. 'As soon as the paper came, my father would say, "Come, take up the paper, and see first of all if George Julian has owt to say this week." George Julian was my father's high priest' (**53**). The readers also spoke back to Harney and the other editors, in their local reports, letters and articles, submitted in their hundreds by people who needed a voice. Chartism became a national movement because each isolated and halting group could send in its piece and see it fitted into the complete national jigsaw puzzle week by week in the pages of the *Northern Star*. Success thereby could breed success, and failure dressed up as success could give heart to failures elsewhere [**doc. 31**]. Like the unstamped, its distribution was in itself a popular movement. Agents for the *Star* and other radical literature, became local organisers and vice versa. The circulation of the paper was sufficient in many areas to provide a living for its local distributor, who might also be paid a little to act as local reporter. In this way the *Star* could provide Chartism with a semi-professional local leadership, a complement to the activities of the local NCA branches (**47b**).

The *Northern Star* was an instant success in commercial as well as political terms. Not only did the subscribers get a handsome return on their money; some of them also eventually got their money back, which was quite unheard of. By January 1838 the circulation had reached 10,000 a week, and a year later – on 26 January 1839 – 17,640 copies were reported sold. At the height of Chartist activity in 1839 the sales rose to between 35,000 and 50,000 a week, the average for the year being 36,000, according to the newspaper stamp returns. This peak was never to be repeated and, in so far as Chartism *was* the *Northern Star*, its circulation can measure the general health of the movement. Stamp returns in 1840 show the circulation halved from that of the previous year, and the steady decline was not even halted in 1842 when an average of 12,500 copies was stamped each week. The low point seems to have been in 1845–46 when sales dropped to under 6,000 (the probable breakeven point for the paper), before rising to about the 1842 level again in 1848 and then dropping away to 5,000 and below in 1850 and 1851. Through most of its career the *Star* was therefore a financial asset to O'Connor, who seems to have poured the money straight back into the movement (**96**).

At $4\frac{1}{2}$d ($1\frac{3}{4}$p) a copy (5d ($2\frac{1}{4}$p) after November 1844), the actual readership of the *Northern Star* is likely to have been far in excess of the numbers sold, for many of the readers were poor men. Impressive though the sales are (compared with a maximum of around 10,000 a week for the *Leeds Mercury*, which was the most successful provincial weekly paper other than the *Star*), the actual circulation must have been even more remarkable. Purchased by groups of workers, or strategically placed in a coffee room or public house, each copy could go through many hands. Those who could not read could listen as others read to them; and all could discuss the ideas put forward week by week. The *Northern Star* brought with it a weekly diet of education, encouragement and advice [**docs 15, 33**] (**21a**).

O'Connor was central to the paper's existence, and it was an important factor in his leadership of Chartism. While in York Castle gaol in 1840–41, it was the *Star* which kept him to the forefront, so that he emerged with his reputation enhanced rather than neglected. But the real strength of the paper was that it was far more than just O'Connor's own journal. Radical editors like William Cobbett and Richard Carlile had had their own papers in the past but, by excluding the voices of their opponents and rivals, these had been driven to start their own papers in response. So the radical press had often deepened the divisions within radicalism. Had the *Northern Star* adopted this policy, it would have fragmented Chartism. Instead the paper was *in*clusive, not exclusive. Opponents of O'Connor, which sometimes included his editors, were given a free voice. G. J. Holyoake's one tribute to O'Connor was that 'In the *Northern Star* he let every rival speak, and had the grand strength of indifference to what anyone said against him in his own columns' (**108**). All aspects of Chartism were reported and discussed, hence all Chartists had to read the *Star* to get a complete picture of what was going on. Far from being a mere mouthpiece for O'Connorism, its success lay in its appeal as *the* paper of Chartism. Even in local areas with their own Chartist papers, the *Northern Star* was read as well, and when these other papers, such as the *Northern Liberator*, failed, the *Star* continued in the dual role of local and national paper, linking the Chartism of 1839–42 with that of 1848.

In appearance the *Northern Star* was a full-sized newspaper in the manner of the *London Dispatch*, the *Leeds Times* or the *Manchester Times*, whereas the unstamped periodicals of the early 1830s and their successors in later radical movements were smaller in size and quite different in their contents. The latter usually had few or no advertisements and carried little news beyond that of their own campaigns; radicals had to read *The Times* or the *Leeds Mercury* for their news, and their own papers for their views. The *Northern Star* combined both functions: its front or second page had the usual collection of small advertisements for patent medicines and the like; then there were pages of general and commercial news, national and local reports, letters, editorials and reviews. Indeed, because the *Star* had so many local reporters, its news coverage was one of the best in the country for the sort of events which interested Chartists. In short, the *Northern Star* was a very good professional newspaper.

Much of this success was due to the editors, especially William Hill who was responsible for the paper until July 1843. Then he and O'Connor parted company over Hill's critical attitude towards the NCA Executive, and the paper was taken over by its publisher, Joshua Hobson, who was soon joined by G. J. Harney as assistant editor. In November 1844, the *Star* was transferred to London, where O'Connor hoped to broaden the basis of its support as *The Northern Star and National Trades Journal*. Hobson sold his Leeds press to the Owenites, who wanted to print their *New Moral World* at their Hampshire community, but he was not happy with London and Harney gradually took over from him. He finally parted from O'Connor over the Land Plan and returned home to his native Huddersfield. Harney continued, assisted by G. A. Fleming (whose *New Moral World* had failed with the Owenite Community in 1845) and Ernest Jones (1847–48), until August 1850. Tensions between Harney and O'Connor over 'red' republicanism were proving too great: William Rider, the veteran Leeds Radical who had been closely involved with the paper from the start, probably wrote most of the leading articles from the autumn of 1849, while Harney devoted his time to his own *Democratic Review of British and Foreign Politics, History and Literature* (June 1849–September 1850) and *Red Republican* (22 June–30 November 1850). By May 1851 Fleming appears to have become editor; he bought the paper from O'Connor for £100 early in 1852, and on 20 March 1852 it appeared under its new ownership as simply the *Star*, a trade union/Owenite/radical paper which still mantained six points, but not the six points of the Charter. Instead the new programme was the broader one of six points of progress – industrial, educational, social, federal, moral and political. In death as in life the *Northern Star* had accurately reflected the general trends within the Chartist movement. A month later the *Star* changed hands again, this time passing to Harney, who issued it for a few more months as the *Star of Freedom*.

With the end of the *Northern Star* at the beginning of 1852 we can mark the end of Chartism. Already in Harney's and Jones's separate papers Chartism had begun to resume that fragmented appearance so common to innumerable radical causes. For just over a brief decade, in the words of its latest historian: 'The *Star* represented a new departure in the history of the working class, in terms of the concentration of the entire strength and variety of a mass movement of working-class protest into the columns of a single national newspaper' (**96**).

10 Rank and File

The Chartist movement may be compared to a public meeting: in the centre, on the platform, stands the national leadership – articulate, politically aware, and readily seen by the historian. Around the platform are clustered the lesser leaders, better known in their regions than nationally, though possible members of one or more of the conventions. Behind them stand the merely local leaders, and at this point the historian's task begins to grow more difficult. Because they operated only in their own local areas, these men rarely emerge into the historical sources, unless they fell foul of the law and ended up in official reports [**docs 14, 15**]. Otherwise the press, and particularly the *Northern Star*, is the main source, with reports of local activities, and lists of local names put forward for the NCA Executive (**38**). Beyond these local stalwarts – the most neglected but most essential constituent part of Chartism or of any popular movement – are gathered the loyal followers, a hard core of dedicated enthusiasts who gave meaning to local activities through thick and thin (**38a**). All these groups might be assumed to have had an ideological commitment to Chartism as a radical concept, but at this point we are still dealing with a small minority of the total population.

Far larger numbers are brought in by the next category, the followers who drifted in and out of the Chartist societies and meetings with the ebb and flow of popular enthusiasm. In 1839, 1842 and 1848 these men and women were eager to sign the petition, to read the *Northern Star*, to cheer O'Connor and to call themselves Chartists, but in 1845 or 1850 they were the ones who melted away, still Chartists in feeling but no part of Chartism at that time. Lastly, and out of ear-shot of the platform, we have the most numerous band of all, working men and women hardly touched, or touched not at all, by Chartism, and whose contact, if any, was only at the fringe of the public meeting, carried there by curiosity rather than conviction.

Any attempt to put numbers on these groups must be a highly speculative undertaking. The signatures on the Charter, allowing for frauds, might suggest that at its height Chartism could in some sense touch around two or three million out of a total adult population in 1841 of about ten million. If each copy of the *Northern Star* at its maximum circulation of around 50,000 copies a week (in 1839) were read by about fifty people (and the figure might well be twenty or a hundred) then the same sort of figure could be reached. That is, Chartism probably appealed to a considerable minority of the population of Britain in the late 1830s and early 1840s, and certainly appealed to a far larger number of people than actually possessed the vote (about 813,000 out of a total population of 18,664,761 in 1841).

Attendance figures at mass meetings are even more speculative. The initial meetings which launched Chartism in Glasgow and Birmingham in 1838 were each reported to have attracted crowds of over 200,000 people. Certainly these were large gatherings, with a two-mile procession in Glasgow with seventy trade unions and forty-eight bands, but in 1841 the total adult population of all Lanarkshire and Renfrewshire was only 300,000; and the adult population of Birmingham and district was only just over 100,000. The Hartshead Moor and Kersal Moor meetings in 1838 were each said to have been attended by 250,000 people, but again these figures seem incredible when set against the total adult populations of the areas. At the 1841 census, the adult population of the West Riding was about 300,000 and the Manchester district contained about 240,000 people over the age of nineteen. William Maccall, an anti-O'Connor Chartist who was living in Bolton between 1837 and 1840, accused O'Connor of lying about the numbers at meetings. There were, he said, not 40,000 to 50,000 present, but only 1,400 to 1,500. What this shows is the inability of the inexperienced eye to estimate the size of a crowd, and Napier was contemptuous of both O'Connor's gross overestimates and the local magistrates' ridiculous underestimates of the numbers involved (**3**).

Some contemporaries were impressed at the way whole populations, men, women and children, appeared to be turning out, often in holiday mood, to these great meetings [**doc. 7**]. The wholesale participation of trade societies with their flags and bands and banners was sufficient to draw huge crowds which could have numbered upwards of 50,000. Of course, not all these people would be Chartists but, as a percentage of the total population, the attendance at these meetings would compare favourably with the turnout at a modern First Division football match.

If this is so, then on grounds of numbers alone Chartism must have been a predominantly working-class movement, appealing largely, though not entirely, to non-electors. The tone of a range of historical sources, from newspaper accounts (friendly and hostile), Home Office reports and criminal records to NCA Executive lists, the autobiographies of participants and the recollections of contemporaries, is working-class – male led but by no means exclusively male [**doc. 24**].

The varying regional strengths and weaknesses of Chartism can in general suggest the nature of this support. Chartism was strongest in areas where domestic industry prevailed, and it appears to have had especial appeal to depressed outworkers in such trades as handloom weaving, framework knitting and nail-making. Among artisans the new engineering trades seem to have furnished less fertile ground than the traditionally radical tailors and shoemakers. Factory workers, with the exception of some skilled spinners, do not bulk large in the records, and the spinners themselves were militant at this time as their skilled monopoly was being broken by the introduction of the self-acting mule (invented 1826). But this evidence should not suggest that Chartism was simply a protest movement by the deprived and the depressed – the last kick of the pre-industrial proletariat. The industrial revolution itself had created large numbers of outworkers, such as the hand-loom weavers who turned the machine-spun yarn into cloth, and they remained an economically important section of the labour force in the 1830s and 1840s. Similarly the industrial revolution had created more jobs for artisans of all kinds, calling on old skills as well as creating new ones. So, beyond economic protest the historian has to look at the traditions of journeyman radicalism and the spread of political ideas in tavern discussion groups and places of work. Though desperation and poverty might have added a violent fringe, and artisans might have added a rational, articulate radicalism, Chartism needs to be seen as a combination and cross-fertilisation of both. No easy generalisations which mechanically identify attitudes with occupations and wage packets will stand up to detailed scrutiny. Often we are left examining the response not of individuals at all, but of communities with living values and traditions (**38a, 86b**).

Something about the nature of Chartism can be learned from a study of the sorts of communities in which it was to be found. There are few examples from purely agricultural areas, where even the village shoe-maker might feel isolated; and in large towns the proportion of Chartists appears to have been small. But in smaller communities Chartism seems to have assumed proportionately greater significance, till in the industrial villages of Lancashire and Yorkshire it does become more appropriate to think of community rather than class. In such villages, where networks of kinship and dependence were close, memories and folk traditions were strong. Many a village around Manchester had its recollections and indeed witnesses of 'Peterloo' (survivors even posed for a photograph in Failsworth to celebrate the passing of the 1884 Reform Act!) (**111**), and in the West Riding the Luddism of 1812 could merge with the 'Plug Plot' riots of 1842 as part of the living experience of ordinary working people (**6**).

Who the Chartists were, and why they were Chartists, are there-fore two deceptively easy and extremely difficult questions to answer. They were printers and newsagents, shopkeepers and tradesmen, weavers and tailors, shoemakers and cordwainers – in short, a cross-section of the working population, but yet not the whole of it. And they came to Chartism to protest and to fight, but also to express their sense of dignity and independence, to claim a right and to express a hope in language tinged with socialism but rooted in the radicalism of the eighteenth and seventeenth centuries and in the Bible. And they were women as well as men, particularly in the early years of mass meetings, demonstrations and riots. Local associations of female Chartists were formed, addressed by women speakers, though it would be unwise to inter-pret this as a precursor of modern feminism. The women were usually fighting for their families and their husbands rather than their own sex as such [**docs 7, 24**] (**38a, 87–87b**).

No individual examples can be typical of this rich variety, yet a few may open windows on to it. Lawrence Pitkethly of Hudders-field, whose name has been mentioned several times in this work, was one of those regional leaders, a little below the front rank. He was a woollen draper, not therefore a working man himself but a small employer of labour (including fellow radical John Leech who managed his shop), who had been enfranchised in 1832. He was a supporter of Richard Carlile, Henry Hetherington and the unstamped; a member of the Huddersfield Political Union in 1832; a leading protester against the sentences passed on the Tolpuddle martyrs and the Glasgow cotton-spinners; the principal associate of Richard Oastler; the leader of the Anti-Poor Law struggle and himself a poor law guardian; the founder of the Huddersfield branch of the Owenite Association of All Classes of All Nations; and the town's most prominent Chartist, being a delegate at the 1839 and 1842 Conventions, and standing with Harney as Chartist candidate for the West Riding at the 1841 general election. As a supporter of O'Connor, he exemplifies the vitality of the local radicalism which gave birth to Chartism (**27, 61**).

Charles Neesom, a prominent second-rank London Chartist, may serve to remind us that Chartists not only involved themselves in other contemporary radical campaigns, but also brought with them the experience of earlier generations. He was born in Scarborough in 1785, and employed as a tailor by a master who was an admirer of Paine. This made Neesom a radical. He came to London in 1810 and involved himself in the radicalism of Cartwright, Cobbett and Hunt. He almost got mixed up in the Spencean Cato Street Conspiracy in 1820, having met Arthur Thistlewood at the Mulberry Tree discussion society in Moorfields. In 1830 he joined class number 40 of the NUWC, worked for Hetherington in the war of the unstamped, joined the LWMA in 1836, and was a founder both of Harney's East London Democratic Association and Lovett's National Association. In 1842 he represented Tower Hamlets at the Complete Suffrage conference in Birmingham, and remained associated with Lovett until 1849. He then joined in the world of militant London secularism in the 1850s, and died in 1861 after a lifetime of radical commitment (**112**).

From the Home Office prison reports we can glimpse Chartists with less well-documented careers. Timothy Higgins, for example, was a redundant cotton-spinner from Ashton-under-Lyne, a victim of the self-acting mule. In 1840 he was aged thirty-five, married, with four children, having been sentenced in 1839 to eighteen months for conspiracy. Intellectually alert, he could read and write, 'has his own ideas upon the subject of religion', was a member of his local Working Men's Association and a republican, and was spending his time in prison writing poetry and improving his arithmetic. Though Scott's novels and common historical works were available in prison, he complained that he had already read all these out of doors 'where I read everything I could find' (**4**). Any account of Chartism as a hunger protest has to find room for such men as Timothy Higgins [**docs 14, 15**]. Finally and more obscurely still, gleanings from obituary notices in radical periodicals of the later nineteenth century throw up such examples as Samuel Collins, 'the bard of Hale Moss' near Oldham, a handloom weaver who was present at 'Peterloo', and supported Cobbett and Hunt but opposed O'Connor's Land Plan; or William Winterbottom of Brighton, who had sold Hetherington's unstamped before becoming a Chartist; or Frederic Riddle, portrait painter of London, who, after a conservative youth, became a Chartist and went on to support the reform movement of the 1860s and the extremist Land and Labour League in the 1870s; or John Hampson of Heywood in Lancashire, a botanist and amateur doctor, who was a consistent supporter of Hunt, Cobbett and O'Connor [**doc. 39**].

For these men Chartism was an experience not to be taken out of context. The older ones had been radicals before 1848; the younger ones were to be radicals again after 1848. Admittedly many so-called Chartists may not have fully entered into the experience, but those who did were to be enriched, as they contributed towards and maintained their own radical values in a truly Chartist culture.

11 Chartist Culture

An over-emphasis on the Six points of the Charter, the agitation to secure these, and its eventual failure, has resulted in an unfortunate neglect of what for many people was the real achievement of Chartism and its true historical significance. For Chartism was not just the dry bones of a political campaign: it was a living experience, without which the politics would have been devoid of content. The Chartists were democrats, and even without their Charter they developed their native, democratic, radical culture which expressed in warm, human terms what political theory alone could never do (**63f, 83b**).

Chartism embodied the values of the working-class world, carried over from the place of work in factory or workshop, and from the place of leisure in public house or club. It nurtured hostility to those outside – the fancy shopkeepers and rich capitalists who considered themselves above the common herd; but at the same time it selected elements from their 'higher' culture and values which it then asserted the democratic right of everyone to share in. It was class-conscious more in the sense of 'us' and 'them' than in any more precise way: the two were separated as much by attitude as by economics, which is why a sense of 'working-class' is always easier to feel than define. This was the common bond which brought educational Chartists like Lovett to the support of the O'Connorites against the Complete Suffragists in 1842: a sense of worthiness, self-respect, and independence based on natural rights, education and mutuality.

This is expressed at all levels of Chartist activity. The great camp meetings on the moors of Lancashire and Yorkshire in the late 1830s and 1840s were following the example of Primitive Methodism in more senses than one (**81**). For these occasions were as much revivals of spirit for Chartists as they were for Methodists. Frank Peel's account of the Hartshead Moor meeting in 1839, for example, conveys the religious sense of the occasion: brass bands and processions, as in the Whitsuntide church and chapel walks; the opening of proceedings with a hymn and a prayer, as in a great religious gathering; the orations of O'Connor and O'Brien (**6**). All fit the expectations and functions of a spiritual occasion, though the gospel of salvation was the Charter. How seriously all Chartists took the parallel is less clear. Ben Wilson of Halifax recalled that, after the opening prayer by William Thornton, Feargus O'Connor laid his hands on his shoulders and said, 'Well done, Thornton, when we get the People's Charter I will see that you are made the Archbishop of York.' The story nicely illustrates O'Connor's touch (**47d**). Yet for many Chartists, Christ had been the first Chartist, so the two were not far apart [**doc. 26**]. Joseph Capper, for example, who was convicted in 1842 for incitement during the riots in the Potteries, was a Primitive Methodist local preacher who had been one of the first converts at the original Mow Cop camp meeting in 1807. He was, it was later recalled, 'a Bible-made man in every function and activity of his life' (**46, 80a**).

The religious model is also applicable to many local meetings, whether taking place in officially named Chartist Churches or not. The larger groups in the localities had the use of their own halls, such as the Carpenters' Hall in Manchester, and smaller groups met in hired rooms, such as that in Humberstone Gate, Leicester, where Thomas Cooper's band of pilgrims met for weekly enlightenment (**43**). Here the weekly, annual and indeed life cycles of ritual were performed. Children were named (pity poor Feargus O'Connor Frost O'Brien McDouall Hunt Taylor, whose forenames bore witness to his parents' zeal, if nothing else); funerals were conducted; Christmas, New Year and Easter celebrated, and saints' days observed (such as Hunt's birthday); in Scotland even marriages could be performed (**83**). Regular Sunday meetings were held in most branches on the one day of rest, when democratic hymns and readings from the *Northern Star* might precede the lecture or discussion (**63f**). The translator of Leon Faucher's *Manchester in 1844* noted that the Carpenters' Hall was 'the Sunday resort of the Chartists. They open and close their meetings with the singing of democratic hymns, and their sermons are political discourses on the justice of democracy and the necessity for obtaining the charter' (**105**).

Few Chartists went as far as many Owenites, or Harney and O'Brien, in rejecting Christianity. Most were probably anticlerical, but regarded Chartism as consistent with the teachings of Christ. Respectable society was thereby attacked with its own values. 'A man may be devout as a Christian, faithful as a friend,' said

William Hill in a pamphlet, 'but if as a citizen he claims rights for himself he refuses to confer upon others, he fails to fulfil the precept of Christ.' As part of the agitation of 1839, Chartists began attending church in large numbers, as at Newcastle, Stockport, Blackburn, and Bolton, where churches were overwhelmed with the presence of working men who did not usually frequent such places. Occasionally there was violence, as at Norwich in 1841 at the dedication of a new church by the bishop, but the good relations enjoyed between W. F. Hook of Leeds and his Chartist church-wardens must also be fitted into the picture. The years 1840 and 1841 also saw the spread of Chartist Churches, first in Scotland and then also in England, at which emphasis was put upon those passages in the Bible conducive to democracy rather than authority (**80, 80a, 81**) [**doc. 26**].

The secular fellowship of the chapel or mechanics' institute was also an integral part of Chartism, with tea meetings, concerts and dancing [**doc. 21**]. Women were encouraged to be active as well as men, and some localities had specific women's groups [**doc. 24**]. Education was another sphere in which some local Chartists were active, though, for practical reasons, there were more evening and Sunday schools than day schools. The burning desire for knowledge filled every Chartist leader and some of their followers. Where the existing schools were alien to working-class ideas, for either religious or political reasons, or where a particularly energetic Chartist teacher was available, schools were set up: the Stalybridge Chartists held a Sunday and day school at the People's Institute in 1839; the Chartist halls in Oldham, Keighley and Hanley included schools; and at a day school at Mottram, five hundred children were taught reading and spelling (**79**). Most of these ventures were ephemeral, but nonetheless important for their members while they lasted. The most outstanding (and untypical) example of intellectual endeavour is to be found at Leicester, where Thomas Cooper showed what his own and Chartism's educational ideals could amount to. Here in 1841 at the Shakespeare Room, Cooper established an adult evening and Sunday school, using the Bible, Channing's *Self Culture* and other such tracts as textbooks. The classes were named after great heroes; Sydney, Marvell and Milton of the seventeenth century, Cartwright and Cobbett of more recent times. They wrote their own Chartist hymns, read Shakespeare and Burns, and heard lectures from Cooper on Milton. But with the depression of 1842 the school declined. The scholars' reaction was now 'What the hell do we care about reading, if we can get nought to eat?' Cooper resorted instead to camp meetings, marches (still with hymn singing), and eventually physical force (**43**).

After 1842 local Chartist community feeling, nurtured by the *Northern Star*, lay at the heart of much residual Chartism [**doc. 33**]. Sunday schools were founded as much as an expression of community solidarity as of educational enterprise (the history of religious Sunday schools was not so different). A common picture might be that presented by the Chartist Rooms in Fig Tree Lane, Sheffield, where Harney took on the local leadership in 1841 and rallied the faithful after their defeats. Here they held their weekly discussions, in a room hung with home-made banners bearing the names of past heroes, and in the presence of a bust of the recently 'martyred' Samuel Holberry; here family teas were held, collections made, hymns sung, and even a Chartist 'litany' recited (**53, 80**).

The experience of such occasions lingered long in the memories of the participants. It was not to be voted away by the House of Commons, or ridiculed out of existence by upper-class society. But several nineteenth-century general historians of their own times, encouraged by Gammage's hostility to O'Connor, dismissed Chartism as a wild and futile gesture which deservedly and contemptuously failed. The complacency of the mid-century Liberal consensus lay heavily over the surviving picture of Chartism. Only with the revival of socialism in England in the 1880s did new interest begin to be shown in what Chartism had really been like (**7**). One of the first reassessments was that of Graham Wallas, biographer of Francis Place, who wrote an article on Chartism in Mrs Annie Besant's periodical, *Our Corner*, in 1888. Mrs Besant was not only a socialist, but also a family friend and admirer of W. P. Roberts, O'Connor's legal adviser. The first major studies since Gammage (which was reissued in 1894), came from John Tildsley in Germany (1898) and Edouard Dolléans in France (1912). Only with the publication of three Columbia University theses (1916), Mark Hovell's posthumous work (1918) and Julius West's posthumous study (1920) can Chartism be said to have been rediscovered by the English-speaking historians. Nevertheless the memory was never lost among the working classes themselves. Ernest Jones remained a popular figure until his death in 1869, and his son Atherley was for long afterwards a favourite guest at the Durham Miners' Gala. 'The blood of the Chartists of forty-eight is the seed of the Reform movement of 1866,' announced the *English Leader* reporting a West Riding reform demonstration addressed by Ernest Jones (**98**); and when, on 6 May 1867, the Reform League called the government's bluff and attended a banned meeting in Hyde Park, both 'Peterloo' and Chartism were in people's minds as the tables were turned on the 'fiasco' of 10 April 1848 (**113**). Ten years later, in 1877, at a demonstration in Newcastle upon Tyne to welcome General Grant to the city, one of the colliery banners proudly bore the likenesses of Feargus O'Connor and Ernest Jones (**114**). Also in the 1870s, with the appearance of autobiographies by Cooper (1872) and Lovett (1876), interest began to revive. As a generation conscious of its history was beginning to slip away, it began to tell its story to the young – not in grand books, but in the obscure columns of working-class periodicals, occasional pamphlets, and local news-papers, especially in contributions sent to W. E. Adams at the *Newcastle Weekly Chronicle* (**45**).

The surviving Chartists had long since abandoned physical force. Some, like Thomas Cooper, seemed reluctant to admit how much they had once favoured it; others looked back with pride, regarding Chartism not as wrong but as necessary in its day but outmoded by developments since then. In most of the later recol-lections there is a note of pride. Like warriors from a long-distant war, the old faithfuls wrote obituary notices for their deceased friends and met to celebrate the continued progress of mankind [**doc. 39**]. At Halifax in 1884 the Reform Act of that year was celebrated at Maude's Temperance Hotel by twenty-two survivors of the old Chartist Association. They were no longer the deprived and the oppressed, but they were not ashamed of the days when they had been. In political terms, they had kept the faith (**47d**).

12   Conclusion

Chartism meant many things to different people, both at the time and since. The perspectives embodied in this book are merely those of one historian and can (and in a seminar should) be challenged in almost every respect, using the contradictory evidence provided in the documentary section. This conclusion aims to set out some of the main lines of interpretation around which discussion should take place.

One major area of controversy concerns the nature of the Chartist movement. The evidence can be interpreted to show that some historians have greatly exaggerated the political aspect of Chartism. Instead, Chartism can be seen as primarily a hunger-protest by the human refuse-tip of the early industrial labour force – the handloom weavers, stockingers and the rest – who wanted food and employment, but voiced their anger and despair through Chartism in the years of economic crisis, 1839–42 and 1848 [**docs 2, 13, 14, 15, 16, 33**]. Without such people Chartism was nothing. The collapse of the movement in the mid-1840s showed it in its true light. Chartism was not a great popular movement – and certainly not a great popular political movement. The mass of the people was largely indifferent to, or oblivious of, the efforts of the leaders, except possibly in the depths of economic hardship. As Disraeli observed in the debate on the Petition in 1839:

> Political rights had so much of an abstract character, their consequences acted so slightly on the multitude, that he did not believe they could ever be the origin of any great popular movement.

This is what G. J. Holyoake called 'the argument of the benevolent but beguiling Tory' [**doc. 40**], and it is found not only in Disraeli but also in Thomas Carlyle [**doc. 16**] and J. R. Stephens [**doc. 2**] who (along with men like Oastler and Owen, as well as many other contemporaries among the higher classes and historians since) argued that the roots of Chartism lay in economic hardship not the lack of political rights. For such men the answer to Chartism was

a solution of what Carlyle called 'the Condition of England Question', and their argument became politically as well as socially
Tory, when they attributed the neglect of the well-being of the
people to the doctrinaire policies of Whig governments in the 1830s
– notably the new Poor Law.

Political radicals, on the other hand, disputed Disraeli's
dismissal of the importance of the 'Rights of Man', and in recent
years historians who regard themselves as politically on the 'Left'
have challenged the established 'Tory' view of Chartism. As
Disraeli was himself acute enough to admit, 'where there were
economical causes for national movements they led to tumult, but
seldom to organisation'. Chartism clearly was organised, using a
political language and political means to demand a political
programme. Could thousands really have attended meetings and
read the *Northern Star*, many of them for over a decade, without
some perceptible impact on their political consciousness, both
collective and individual, whatever their original motivation? Why
should out-of-work handworkers (usually regarded as more literate
than factory workers) be dismissed as ignorant just because they
were also hungry? This is the view filtered through sources written
by upper-class educationalists and moralisers, not the one which
emerges from a reading of the *Northern Star*, prison interviews and
Chartist autobiographies.

Central to this discussion of how political were the Chartists is
the lament of Thomas Cooper at the end of his autobiography that
'working men had ceased to think, and wanted to hear no
thoughtful talk' [**doc. 41**]. Whether or not he was right in his judgment of working men in 1870, was he merely indulging in romantic
nostalgia when he recalled the Chartist days (a charge often
brought against some historians who share Cooper's view), or had
something remarkable happened in the 1830s and 1840s to enable
political radicals to exploit the severe economic and social distress
of early industrial Britain and thus to produce the first large-scale
politically conscious movement among the emerging working
classes?

One recent contribution to this debate (**82a**) suggests that this
latter is indeed possible. Bronterre O'Brien once wrote

> Knaves will tell you, that it is because you have no property that
> you are unrepresented. I tell you, on the contrary, it is because
> you are unrepresented that you have no property (**55**).

A generation of working people, overworked or unemployed, ill-paid, badly housed, de-skilled, exploited and suffering from what were seen as the effects of the Whig 'class' legislation of the 1830s, believed this argument. Thus, while Chartism had its roots in social and economic conditions, it was essentially a political movement. A struggle was taking place about control in the workplace, in leisure, in education and in religion. Chartism offered a programme for hope to those who saw themselves as victims of the power and control exerted by the enfranchised classes over the unenfranchised.

Such an interpretation can also throw new light on the problem of why Chartism failed. A rather mechanical economic interpretation of the movement, such as that offered by Rostow's 'social tension chart', provides an equally mechanical explanation of Chartist failure, attributing it to the improvement in economic conditions after 1842 and, especially, after 1848. Other historians, following Place, Lovett, Gammage and other contemporaries, have attributed Chartist failure to O'Connor's leadership and bad organisation [**doc. 42**]. A recent development has been to stress the view that Chartism did not so much fail as suffer defeat, both ideological and military, at the hands of a confident and powerful state (**97b**). Not wholly compatible with this is the latest view which argues that, if Chartism was based on a juncture of economic, social and political attitudes, its failure can be explained by the divergence of these attitudes once the Chartist message had proved false. Radicals had offered a unique solution to the problems of the 1830s. Not only were they unable to implement their political solution, being shown to be impotent in 1839, 1842 and again in 1848; but also conditions did begin to improve even without the Charter. The Mines Act (1842), Factory Acts (1844, 1847), repeal of the Corn Laws (1846), abolition of the Poor Law Commission (though not of the hated Act) (1847) and Public Health legislation (1848) all proved that a restricted franchise did not necessarily mean the oppression of the people. Thus the 'Tory' interpretation of Chartism appears to gain some credence from the policies of Sir Robert Peel and successor ministries after 1841 (**82a**).

Far from being a cause of Chartism's failure, such Acts have sometimes been seen as one of the movement's successes. Indeed Chartism did make a powerful political impact, bringing a new urgency to the philanthropic impulses of private individuals and the reforming tendencies of those in government – though to the list of social reforms should be added the introduction and implementation of legislation extending police forces to many parts of the provinces, a Chartist achievement but never a Chartist aim! The quest for Chartist achievement has also led sometimes to a listing of enactments of the later nineteenth and twentieth centuries, by which many points of the Charter were granted, but this seems fallacious. Those Acts cannot even remotely be attributed to Chartist pressure, and the real spirit of democracy which lay behind the points of the Charter remains unrealised even in the later twentieth century (**38a, 83b**). The positive achievements of the Chartists are to be found not in legislation, passed at the time or in the remoter future, but in the mobilisation of the considerable mental, spiritual and emotional capacities of the working men and women of early industrial Britain [**doc. 42**]. The Chartists' greatest achievement was Chartism, a movement shot through not with despair but with hope.

Part Four: Documents

The People's Charter

document 1

The draft parliamentary Bill, known as the 'People's Charter', was finally approved by the London Working Men's Association on 8 May 1838. This minute of their proceedings a week later describes the arrangements made for putting the Charter forward at the Glasgow meeting on 21 May, along with the Birmingham Political Union's National Petition.

On a motion by Hartwell and Lawrence the following resolution was agreed to,

Resolved, That the Members of the Working Men's Association fully concurring in the great principles of Universal Suffrage, Annual Parliaments, the Ballot, and all the other essentials to the free exercise of Man's political rights – and hearing that a meeting is to be held at Glasgow on the 21st of May in furtherance of those objects do request our Honorary Members Mr Thos. Murphy and the Revd Dr Wade to present to that meeting our pamphlet entitled the 'People's Charter' being the outline of an act to provide for the just representation of the people of Great Britain in the Commons House of Parliament – embracing the principles of Universal Suffrage, No Property Qualifications, Annual Parliaments, Equal Representation, Payment of Members, and Vote by Ballot prepared by a committee of twelve persons six members of parliament and six members of the Working Men's Association.

Working Men's Association Minutes, vol. I, 1837–1839, minute for 15 May, 1838, British Library, Add. Mss 37,773 f. 107.

A knife and fork question

document 2

Joseph Rayner Stephens, an independent Methodist minister and turbulent opponent of the New Poor Law and the factory masters, was one of the most popular leaders in the North. His political theory is somewhat confused, but generally seems to fall into that category described by G. J. Holyoake [**doc. 40**] *as Tory. The occasion of this speech was the great Kersal Moor meeting, near Manchester, to elect delegates on 24 September 1838.*

. . . They were to tell all those who had hitherto withstood them, and trifled with them and affected to despise and scorn them – they were there to tell their foes throughout the land that they were mighty, because they knew their rights, and had the power as well as the will to obtain them. (Cheers.) The principle of the Resolution, therefore, which he had risen to speak to, was a principle which every man was obliged to acknowledge in argument, though he affected to disregard it, – the principle which acknowledged the right of every man that breathed God's free air and trod God's free earth, to have his home and his hearth, and his wife and his children, as securely guaranteed to him as of any other man whom the Aristocracy had created. (Cheers.) This question of Universal Suffrage was a knife and fork question after all; this question was a bread and cheese question, notwithstanding all that had been said against it; and if any man ask him what he meant by Universal Suffrage, he would answer, that every working man in the land had a right to have a good coat to his back, a comfortable abode in which to shelter himself and his family, a good dinner upon his table, and no more work than was necessary for keeping him in health, and as much wages for that work as would keep him in plenty, and afford him the enjoyment of all the blessings of life which a reasonable man could desire. (Tremendous cheers).

Northern Star, 29 September, 1838.

The Ashburton Working Men's Association
document 3

Although the London Working Men's Association was a small body, it was accepted as parent by many similar small associations which grew up in the country. Here we witness the birth of one such local society in February 1839. This letter is evidently written by a poorly educated man on behalf of a few friends who, in the face of considerable odds, had managed to create quite a stir in their town. But the question for the historian is, should the size of Chartism be reckoned by the small membership of the Working Men's Association, unable to afford the National Rent to support their delegate or to supply a speaker of their own, or should it be measured by the 2000 people who attended the public demonstration?

With this you will recieved the National Petition from Ashburton in the county of Devon – The Working Men's Association has been forme'd only a few weeks and on account of two strong factions Whig & Tory we have to fight against we thought it prudent to have a Public Demonstration here, and as we were destitute of speakers we have been to a great expense in having Mr Wm Webber, from Brixham and other speakers from Totnes and other towns, we had a Public Demonstration here last Evening and the people's Charter was ably explained by these speakers there were 2000 persons present as our funds are very low we are compeled to put of sending the National Rent for a few weeks but we will do our utmost endeavours to get the most we can and it shall be forwarded to its proper quarters [*sic*].

Samuel Mann, John Ball Lee and Wm Maunder to John Collins, 27 February 1839, in *General Convention of the Industrial Classes, 1839* letter-book in Place Collection, British Library, Add. Mss 34, 245, f. 75.

document 4

Extremism from the London Democratic Association

While the Convention was deliberating strategy, Harney's Democratic Association was urging militant action through those delegates who believed in such 'ulterior measures' as the 'sacred month' of general strike. The following resolution was carried unanimously at a public meeting held by the LDA at the City Road Hall of Science on 28 February 1839, with Harney in the Chair.

Moved by _____ Coombe, seconded by Joseph Fisher – Resolved – That this meeting is of opinion that the Peoples Charter could be established as the law of the land, within one month from the present time, provided the people and their leaders do their duty, and this meeting is further of opinion, that it is essentially just, and indispensably necessary to meet all acts of oppression, with immediate resistance.

It was further unanimously resolved on the motion of William

Ryder, seconded by Richard Marsden – Resolved That this meeting convey to the General Convention, their opinion that for the due discharge of the duties of the Convention it is essentially necessary, that there be no delay, except what may be absolutely necessary in the presentation of the National Petition, and we hold it to be the duty of the Convention, to impress upon the people the necessity of an immediate preparation for ulterior measures.

Cornelius Bentley and Thos. Moore to William Lovett, Secretary to the General Convention, in *General Convention of the Industrial Classes, 1839*, letter-book in Place Collection, British Library, Add. Mss 34, 245 ff. 76–77.

document 5
The National Convention

The Convention, especially in its early stages, scarcely had the appearance of a revolutionary body.

. . . We left the National Assembly Hall impressed with a very high admiration of the business-like, quiet, and respectable manner in which all their proceedings were carried on, and the spirit which pervaded the assembly. It was evident that a class of elderly, bald-headed men, of whom one of the delegates from Lancashire may be mentioned as a good specimen, are the brains of the Convention, and direct everything except its tongue. The tongue, however, was always an unruly member, and they have provided against this as well as they can by resolving that they will not collectively be held answerable for what any member may say.

'A visit to the National Convention', *The Chartist*, 12 March, 1839.

document 6
Physical and moral force

Following the Llanidloes riot on 30 April, the moderate Chartist *delivered this solemn editorial on the subject of physical force. Though firmly on the moral force side, this extract illustrates the complexity of the views which could be held and which makes nonsense of any attempt to categorise too rigidly the moral and physical force positions.*

That Englishmen have a right, *in extreme cases*, to have recourse to physical force to free themselves from an unendurable tyranny, is a truth so important and so undisputed that it forms the very foundation of our system of government. It is not only admitted, but it is even asserted, reiterated, defended, and justified, by the most zealous of the Tory writers upon the Constitution of this country . . .

But although this is upon all sides admitted, it is also upon all sides agreed that this is a fearful remedy, which, like hazardous, extreme, and painful operations in surgery, is only to be brought into action in very extreme cases, when all ordinary courses of treatment have failed. Physical force is a thing not to be lightly had recourse to; it is the last remedy known to the Constitution. . . .

. . . Nothing but a simultaneous rising at the same hour all over the kingdom could give you a *chance* of success by arms – even that would give you but a slender chance, and that you *cannot* effect. Retain your arms then, for it is possible that you may have to use them in your own defence, with the law and the Constitution upon your side. But use them not until that time comes. Pursue the course of *peaceful* agitation – press forward your great cause under the watchwords of 'Peace, Law, Order'. It may be delayed, but it must prevail. Continue these acts of buccaneering folly, *and you and your children are slaves for ever.*

'The first essay in physical force', *The Chartist*, 12 May, 1839.

document 7
Kersal Moor, 1839

Before the Kersal Moor meeting in May 1839, the military commander, Napier, had been worried that his forces would not be strong enough to overawe the Chartists and so prevent a disturbance. In the event, a skilful deployment of forces proved to be sufficient, and the day passed off quietly. Feargus O'Connor claimed that a quarter of a million people were present. Napier was confident that his own estimate was the correct one.

I have been on Kersal Moor in the meeting and around the meeting, and will stake my life on it that there are not thirty thousand people, of which at least one *fourth* are bonnets and quantities of children. When I left the ground the chief speakers appeared to have left the meetings. What the great Orator *Beer* may do towards Evening I cannot say but I have not the slightest apprehension that any great thing will take place that the Constables cannot quash straight without our assistance. I shall keep this open till the latest train.

5 o Clock – all perfectly quiet.

Sir Charles James Napier to the Home Office, '¼ past two P.M.' 25 May, 1839, PRO, HO 40/53.

document 8

The weakness of London

The disappointing level of the Chartist response in London was widely discussed during the 1839 Convention. If the following account is a fair one, then what interpretation of Chartism does this suggest, and was the paper (which was published in London) justified in its optimism about the provinces? Note the appreciation of London in the Chartists' strategy.

It is of no use to refuse to look our difficulties in the face. The fact is, that, be it from listlessness, ignorance, want of thought, incapacity to reason as to political causes and effects, or satisfaction with things as they are, the great majority of the working men of the metropolis are altogether indifferent as to representation. They feel certain evils, and they complain of them, but they do not apply themselves to consider whence they proceed.

In the country, we believe, it is far otherwise . . . . We are sorry to have to report that in the metropolis, where the lead should have been taken, there is nothing doing; and unless the metropolis be set working, all agitation elsewhere is useless. It is here that the seat of Government is. A demonstration in the streets of London comes before the very eyes of those who make the laws. An atmosphere of agitation here does not dissipate without first involving the two houses of legislation in its influence. A hundred demonstrations in the country are only heard of through the newspapers of the factions, which invariably describe them as contemptible, diminish the numbers, and caricature the speeches.

'Prospects of our cause', *The Chartist*, 30 June, 1839.

document 9

The Birmingham Bull Ring riots, July 1839

*Though Birmingham was usually a centre of moderation (**71**), in the summer
of 1839 violence erupted, with the local magistrates (including members of
the BPU) on one side and the bulk of the Chartists on the other. In the riots
described here, Dr Taylor and Peter McDouall were arrested, which
prompted the resolutions of the Convention for which Lovett and Collins were
arrested [**doc. 10**].*

The national convention was then holding its sittings in that city,
and contributed great activity to the motions of the chartists, who
made a practice of assembling in great numbers every evening on
the open place called the Bull-ring. On the 5th of July these
disorderly persons met as usual in the great square. The borough
magistrates, however, who had for some days been in constant
communication with the home-office, had by this time bespoken
a picked body of sixty policemen from the metropolis. The railway
train delivered them at Birmingham that evening, and without
even waiting for the cooperation of the military, they proceeded
immediately to the scene of confusion. They began by directing the
people to disperse, but when this injunction was seen to take no
effect, the police filed off four abreast, and made for the monument
of lord Nelson which stood in the centre of the Bull-ring, set round
with the flags of the convention. These they succeeded in
capturing, but the mob, who had been at first disconcerted by the
impetuosity of the charge, when they beheld their ensigns one of
which bore a death's head in the hands of the enemy, made a
desperate return, recovered the contested banners, broke the poles
up into short sticks, and after a fierce and indiscriminate combat
in which several of the policemen who were only armed with
staves, were seriously hurt, and more than one man stabbed, the
chartists began at length to obtain the advantage.

Fortunately, however, at this juncture, the 4th dragoons arrived
on the spot. Riding by concert up every avenue which led to the
place, they completely inclosed the Bullring. The appearance of the
military was the signal for the people to disperse, and the routed
mob proceeded with the cavalry in close pursuit down Digbeth and
up Bromsgrove-street to St Thomas's Church. Here they tore up
the pallisades, and for a moment made a stand. But the tumult was
eventually reduced, by midnight the streets were comparatively

quiet, and the military planting a guard in the great square retired to their barracks.

Annual Register, 1839, p. 305.

document 10
The cause of Lovett's arrest in Birmingham

The following protest at the behaviour of the police in the Bull Ring riots was placarded in the streets, resulting in the arrest of Lovett, and of John Collins who took the resolutions to be printed. Lovett's insistence on taking full responsibility is one of the nobler and more courageous acts of Chartism and important in weighing up a defence of his character against rivals who subsequently condemned him for his faith in moral force.

In consequence of the disturbed state of the town, and the arrests which had taken place, the Convention held a meeting at an early hour, and Mr Richards having been appointed to the chair, and Mr Lovett, secretary, the following resolutions were proposed, seconded, and carried without a dissentient voice; and a number of copies were ordered to be printed for immediate circulation in the town of Birmingham:

'That this Convention is of opinion that a wanton, flagrant, and unjust outrage has been made upon the people of Birmingham by a bloodthirsty and unconstitutional force from London, acting under the authority of men who, when out of office, sanctioned and took part in the meetings of the people; and now, when they share in public plunder, seek to keep the people in social slavery and political degradation.'

'That the people of Birmingham are the best judges of their own right to meet in the Bull Ring, or elsewhere – have their own feelings to consult respecting the outrage given, and are the best judges of their own power and resources in order to obtain justice.'

'That the summary and despotic arrest of Dr Taylor, our respected colleague, affords another convincing proof of the absence of all justice in England, and clearly shows that there is no security for life, liberty, or property, till the people have some control over the laws which they are called upon to obey.'

By order,

WM. LOVETT, Secretary.

The delegates present having intimated that it would be better for each of them to sign their name to the resolutions,

MR LOVETT said that he thought they could not spare any of them to become victims; one sacrifice was sufficient, and therefore he alone would put his name to them.

'General Convention, Friday, July 5', *Northern Star*, 13 July, 1839.

document 11

The Newport rising, November 1839

The following extract from evidence given at the trial of John Frost illustrates the difficulties involved in trying to arrive at any coherent picture of what really happened. The witness is certain that the Chartists had come to demand the release of prisoners, not to start a general rising – a view not supported by witnesses for the prosecution.

Edward Patton, a carpenter of Newport, deposed as follows: The parcel of people I saw in the morning of the riot, were armed; they had guns, sticks, etc.; the sticks had iron points, I did not see many with guns. I saw of this body two hundred or three hundred. There were not many more. I had full view of those on Stowe Hill. I was a little bit alarmed, but not particularly so, but I wished to see what they would say and do. I was never at a chartist lodge. I did not know what they came to do. I was not at work that morning. I did not hear that they were to come down from the hills. I believe that a great number of them went to the gates from the hotel. I know the two bow-windows in front of the Westgate. I never saw anything done to the windows of the Westgate. I did not hear a crash of the windows. They were not very tumultuous. They drew up in front of the Westgate. I am certain they said that the prisoners were taken before daylight. It was about nine o'clock in the morning when they came down Stowe Hill. It was broad daylight two hours before that. Those that were in the Westgate were taken before daylight. The body of the mob stood for a space, and asked for the prisoners who were taken before daylight. None of the mob went forward as spokesmen. They came close to the door. I could only see the steps, to which the mob came close up. The first moment or two they asked for the prisoner Smith; then a rush was made. Then I heard firing, and took to my heels. I cannot say whether the mob had guns, pikes or clubs. I cannot tell whether they were armed for the biggest part. I heard some one say, in a very loud voice, 'No, never.' I was distant from the door of the Westgate twenty-five yards when I heard the words. I heard no groaning. I could not say where the firing began. No man could judge. You nor I could not tell. Saw no smoke outside. It is likely enough the firing began from the Westgate inn . . . .

Annual Register, 1840 (Appendix to the Chronicle, Law Cases, &c), pp. 215–216.

Law and order after Newport
document 12

Before the completion of the railway network, the forces of law and order were severely restricted in their mobility, as the following letter from the Home Office illustrates on the day after the Newport rising.

I hasten to acknowledge the receipt of a letter . . . reporting the attack made upon the Town of Newport by a large body of Chartists from the neighbouring Country & to inform you that I have lost no time in communicating with the military authorities, and an arrangement has been made for the immediate march of eight companies of the 45th Regt from Winchester for the district in which the deplorable event has occurred. Orders have been already despatched for their march and they will probably arrive at Bristol on the 10th Inst. & can of course if necessary cross over by steamer to Newport the same evening. Two guns with a proportion of gunners have also been ordered from Woolwich to Monmouth. They will proceed by railroad to Twyford from there by forced marches to Bristol. I regret much that there are no troops stationed at any nearer points that would be available for this service but I think that the check which these insurgents have received from the firmness of the inhabitants of Newport & the small body of troops stationed in the town, together with the active measures taken by the Magistrates will have induced their dispersion for the time & the presence of the large force which will arrive in the course of a few days [*will*] be sufficient to maintain future tranquility.

Home Office to the Mayor of Newport, 5 November, 1839, PRO, HO 41/15.

document 13
The poor in Nottingham, 1839

*Charles Napier was sympathetic towards the Chartists and, while determined
to maintain law and order, he was rarely in doubt as to the outcome of any
clash between his troops and the Chartists, who were more to be pitied than
feared. Like many sympathisers from the higher classes, he attributed much
of the troubles to the new poor law.*

Journal, December 1st – An anonymous letter come, with a Chartist plan. Poor creatures, their threats of attack are miserable. With
half a cartridge, and half a pike, with no money, no discipline, no
skilful leaders, they would attack men with leaders money and
discipline, well armed, and having sixty rounds a man. Poor men!
A republic! What good did a republic ever do? What good will it
ever do?

2nd – The streets of this town are horrible. The poor starving
people go about by twenties and forties, begging, but without the
least insolence; and yet some rich villains, and some foolish
women, choose to say they try to extort charity. It is a lie, an
infernal lie, neither more nor less: – nothing can exceed the good
behaviour of these poor people, except it be their cruel sufferings.

3rd – Spoke to the mayor about a subscription: – the excellent
mayor, Mr Roworth. He joins me in all my opinions as to the
thrice-accursed new poor law, its bastiles, and its guardians. Lying
title! They guard nothing, not even their own carcasses, for they
so outrage misery that if a civil war comes they will be immediately
sacrificed.

W. Napier (**3**), II, pp. 93–4.

document 14
A Chartist prisoner

*In order to be able to answer parliamentary questions about the treatment of
Chartist prisoners, the Home Office was supplied by its inspectors of prisons,
led by Captain W. J. Williams, with detailed reports on each of the seventy-
three Chartists still serving sentences during the winter of 1840–41. The
following is one example from the notebook into which the reports were copied.
See also (**4**) and [**doc. 15**].*

Prison, in which undergoing sentence. County Gaol at Chester

Name and Age	*Charles Davies* – aged 26
Married or Single – *Number of Children*	Married. no family
Religious Persuasion ...	Calls himself a Calvinist
Instruction	Very limited – but has considerably improved himself and is a man of considerable energy and talent.
Profession or Trade	Cotton spinner by business – When apprehended was keeping a shop for the sale of periodical publications and newspapers at Stockport.
Condition in Life, and *means of Subsistence*	Dependent upon his own exertions. In consequence of taking an active part against the masters on the subject of Wages and being a delegate from the Working Men has been unable to get work for two years
Offence	Conspiracy
Sentence, and Date and *Place of Conviction*	Committed at the Autumn assizes 1839 at Chester and sentenced to be Impd 18 Calr months and find Sureties himself in £500 and two in £100 each to keep the peace for 5 years longer.
Length of Imprisonment *before Trial*	5 days
Expiration of *Sentence*	February 10th 1841
Ordinary Diet of the *Prisoners' Class to* *which Prisoner* *belongs*	1 lb bread daily, 1 quart of gruel at breakfast, $1\frac{1}{2}$ lbs of potatoes at dinner, 1 quart of gruel for supper
Extra Diet, when *allowed*	Allowed to purchase
General Treatment	Complains of the want of meat. has had a trifle sent him from without. his wife £2 from the Victim Fund.
Present and Ordinary *State of Health – if* *predisposed to Chronic* *Disease, effect of* *Imprisonment*	(Surgeon's Report to Inspector.) Has had a severe attack of inflammation of the throat and tonsils – a complaint to which he was previously liable – in Feb. last. He occasionally complains of some

slight chest symptoms and seems to
suffer in some degree from his
confinement.

Conduct in Prison ...... No complaint

Observations of the Inspector on the foregoing Case.
Davies. This man's Political agitation seems to have emanated from
the failure of his attempts to increase the wages of the Working
Men, which he says that Political power can only accomplish. I
find among the notes of a long conversation with him the following
words 'The great distress is the cause of our discontent – if the
wages were what they ought to be, we should not hear a word
about the suffrage. If the masters will only do something for the
Workmen to get them the common comforts of life, we should be
the most contented creatures upon earth.' I have no doubt this
man would go *any lengths* to carry out his own feelings with regard
to the working classes.

(*signed*) W. J. Williams
Inspr of Prisons 30 Octr 1840.

PRO, HO 20/10.

document 15

The Bradford rising, 1840

From the interviews with Chartist prisoners conducted by W. J. Williams
[**doc. 14**] *comes the following reported account (possibly biased by the*
circumstances) of participation in the attempted rising in Bradford in January
1840. The prisoner was Emanuel Hutton, aged twenty-eight, a married man
with two children, who had been convicted at the York Spring Assizes of riot
and sentenced to eighteen months' hard labour at Wakefield gaol. He was a
woolcomber, 'much distressed' and earning an average of only five shillings
a week; he was able to read but not write, was in delicate health, and claimed
to belong to the Church of England.

I was called up at night and when I came down a gun was put
into my hands. I don't know who gave it to me. I wish I had. If
I had known it at York it would have been told. I went down stairs
and saw a man who told me to follow him – I did so for about 200
yards and there saw a lot of men who bade me to go into the
market place with them – one gave me the Gun. I asked several

questions – there seemed no one appointed to lead. We went into the market place and as soon as I saw the Constables I set off – but was caught. I had been at the Meetings. I was a Chartist by reading the Star Newspaper. I had heard my neighbors talk of a rising – they had fixed many a day. I was no physical Force Chartist altho' there is sorry appearance of it I own. I will take care I do not get into prison again for such an offence – it will learn me experience.

Report of W. J. Williams on Emanuel Hutton, 23 December, 1840, PRO, HO 20/10.

Carlyle on Chartism

document 16

Thomas Carlyle was the foremost social critic of his age. He had little time for radicalism but even less for the modern world which had created what he called 'the Condition of England question'. Another relevant phrase which he coined was the 'cash nexus' to describe the dehumanised social relations of his age. His outlook was fundamentally conservative.

We are aware that, according to the newspapers, Chartism is extinct. . . . So say the newspapers; – and yet, alas, most readers of newspapers know withal that it is indeed the 'chimera' of Chartism, not the reality, which has been put down. The distracted incoherent embodiment of Chartism, whereby in late months it took shape and became visible, this has been put down; or rather has fallen down and gone assunder by gravitation and law of nature: but the living essence of Chartism has not been put down. Chartism means the bitter discontent grown fierce and mad, the wrong condition therefore or the wrong disposition, of the Working Classes of England. It is a new name for a thing which has had many names, which will yet have many.

Thomas Carlyle, *Chartism*, second edition, 1842, p. 2.

'The Lion of Freedom'

document 17

Thomas Cooper, who at this stage in his career was a fervid admirer of

Feargus O'Connor, was believed to have written the following poem to commemorate O'Connor's release from York Castle gaol in 1841. Thereafter it became a favourite song with Chartist crowds whenever Feargus appeared. Cooper later denied his authorship (43).

The lion of freedom comes from his den,
We'll rally around him again and again,
We'll crown him with laurels our champion to be,
O'Connor, the patriot of sweet liberty.

The pride of the nation, he's noble and brave
He's the terror of tyrants, the friend of the slave,
The bright star of freedom, the noblest of men,
We'll rally around him again and again.

Though proud daring tyrants his body confined,
They never could alter his generous mind;
We'll hail our caged lion, now free from his den,
And we'll rally around him again and again.

Who strove for the patriots? was up night and day?
And saved them from falling to tyrants a prey?
It was Feargus O'Connor was diligent then!
We'll rally around him again and again.

Northern Star, 11 September, 1841.

document 18
The riot at O'Connor's lecture, Manchester 1842

Newspaper reports are important sources for the historian, but they have many drawbacks. Even when they agree on the main facts which they report, their emphases can be so different as to raise doubts as to whether the differing accounts really are of the same occurrence. The riot which broke out at the Manchester Hall of Science at O'Connor's lecture on 8 March 1842, was reported by the millowners' Manchester Guardian in a manner not entirely to the Chartists' and O'Connor's credit.

On Monday evening last, Mr Feargus O'Connor delivered the first of three lectures, in the building called the Mechanics' Hall of Science, Campfield; and the large hall was crowded. It was publicly announced that his next lecture, on the following evening, would be on the subject of the repeal of the legislative union with Ireland; and last evening was the time appointed for this lecture. There was a tolerably large attendance, though not so numerous as that of the preceding evening; and it is alleged by the chartists, that about a hundred men, most of whom they say were provided with sticks, forced their way into the room without paying the pence required for admission at the doors. . . . The chartists proposed that Mr James Scholefield should take the chair; the adverse party opposed this, and proposed another chairman. The question was put to the vote, and each party contended that they were in the majority. There were mixed up with this cause of contention, sundry cries about the corn-laws, and many persons wished the discussion to be on that subject instead of the repeal of the union. This of course increased the confusion, and, as the chartists appeared determined to place Mr Scholefield in the chair, the opposite party proceeded from words to blows; the rails, benches, bannisters, gas-pipes, &c. in the hall were torn up, and speedily converted into offensive weapons; and, thus armed, an attack was made upon the chartists, who were speedily driven from the room. Mr O'Connor, it is said, made a prompt exit through a back door, on the beginning of the fray. Several persons are stated to have been much hurt, and we were told that one of the reporters received a severe blow on the head.

'Mr Feargus O'Connor. – Row in the "Hall of Science".', *Manchester Guardian*, 9 March, 1842.

Another view of the riot   **document 19**

The Northern Star, *in contrast to the above quotation from the* Manchester Guardian, *was completely sure that the Chartists were the innocent party. O'Connor's own account of his involvement shows him to have been the brave leader that he knew himself to be.*

The missiles now began to fly in all directions at those on the platform, when I went in front, took off my hat, and cheered the Chartists on. While I was in the act of cheering, four or five of the Chartists – young Campbell being the only one I knew – rushed to the front, and seizing me by the collar and body, attempted to

back, saying, 'Feargus, they'll murder you, that's what
come here for.' As they were in the act of pulling me
in, I received a blow of a large stone on the left shin, that
knocked me down on a bench. I got up, and now stones, from a
pound to three pound weight, pieces of iron and missiles of all
descriptions began to fly round me. Whittaker and two or three
others seized me by the collar, and while dragging me back, I
received a blow of a stone on the breast and one in the neck. I then
turned round to those who held me, and said, 'for God's sake let
me loose, I must jump down.' Just as I turned round I received
a blow of some sharp instrument behind, which cut my hat
through, and as I fronted the meeting again, I received a tremendous blow from a large stone just above the right eye, which
knocked me down, the blood gushing out copiously. Higgin-
bottom, Whittaker, and two or three lifted me up and dragged me
off the platform.

'Bloody and ferocious attack of a band of assassins, hired by the
League, upon Feargus O'Connor and the Chartists of Manchester',
Northern Star, 12 March, 1842.

Manchester in 1842

document 20

*The annual reports of the Ministry to the Poor in Manchester, a Unitarian
organisation, give a detailed personal view of the lives of the poor. This
extract illustrates why the idea of a general strike was impracticable, and
describes the practical necessity which compelled workers to stay at work
unless physically prevented by the strike leaders. Compare this extract with
the scenes described in Mrs Gaskell's* Mary Barton (**102**). *Her husband was
president of the Ministry to the Poor at this time. What follows relates to
the events of July and August 1842.*

The demand for soup tickets continues unabated, and the very
early hour at which many persons are accustomed to resort to the
kitchen in Bale-street proves the extremity of their destitution. I
was lately conversing with a poor man, who has a wife, three sons
and a daughter, all of whom except the woman were then out of
work, and he informed me that being unable to sleep or rest, he
went for soup one morning so early as half-past one o'clock, and
even then found 50 or 60 persons before him. At the time referred

to in the above statement, though the more skilled of the hand-loom weavers and the out-door labourers had pretty regular employment, yet many other classes were suffering unusual depression. Such was the case with factory operatives and mechanics, and there were numbers of dyers, spinners, and the more common descriptions of weavers, who had long had nothing to do. I was myself acquainted with many individuals connected with these branches of industry, who had been almost without any work for periods varying from a few weeks to twelve months. When to all this is added the long-continued depreciation of wages, we shall be convinced that the measure of human endurance was filled to the brim.

At length this measure was exceeded, and the waters of civil strife and commotion threatened to overflow the land, and sweep away the institutions of society. In the month of August, the general turn-out occurred. Such a course, however, only added to the existing distress, and involved many families in great difficulties and privations. This was peculiarly hard in the case of those who were kept out of employment by intimidation. I met with a considerable number of cases of this description, and will mention one of them. A poor calico-weaver, whose family consisted of five individuals, had himself been nearly without work ever since Whitsuntide, and was chiefly dependent on his eldest daughter, who wrought at a power-loom factory, where they had for some time been employed but three or four days per week. When, therefore, she was kept entirely from her usual employment for several weeks in succession, the whole family were deprived of a sufficiency of the common necessaries of life, and were in danger of being ejected by the landlord from the house to which they had but lately removed. Yet these poor people are of remarkably peaceable habits, and would have been glad to have worked if they had been allowed.

John Layhe's ninth *Annual Report of the Ministry to the Poor*, 30 April, 1843, pp. 7–8.

document 21

Chartist leisure

Leisuretime activities were an important part of Chartist life, and not even the general strike of August 1842 could cause more than a minor interruption to the planned programme of celebrations to mark the anniversary of the Peterloo massacre, on 16 August 1842. But contrast this scene with the contemporary one described in doc. 20. What does this imply about Chartism?

Last evening, a Chartist tea party and ball, as previously announced by placard, were given in the Carpenters' Hall, by 'The committee for the erection of Hunt's monument'. The room and gallery were densely crowded, and an amateur band was in attendance. John Murray presided. After tea, the Rev. James Scholefield entered the room, and announced that Mr Feargus O'Connor was unable to attend, as he was, in conjunction with other Chartists, engaged in considering what measures were best to be adopted in the present crisis. Several Chartist sentiments were then proposed from the chair, and responded to by some operatives, and a few songs were sung; after which dancing commenced and was kept up till a late hour.

Leeds Mercury, 20 August, 1842, supplement.

document 22

The Holiday Insurrection, August 1842

The Leeds Mercury *was the voice of the West Riding millowners, and its editor, Edward Baines, had no doubt that the so-called 'Plug Plot' riots were the consequence of Chartist agitators taking advantage of industrial depression to mislead the working people into fruitless action contrary to all the dictates of sound political economy.*

Our columns are filled with particulars of the strangest and wildest *Holiday-Insurrection* that has ever been attempted; an *Insurrection* conducted in the name of '*peace, law, and order!*' – an Insurrection the most extensive, yet in some respects the most harmless, known in the modern history of England: – an Insurrection more foolish than wicked in the dupes who have caught the contagion, but we fear much more wicked than foolish in the leaders who planned it. . . .

If any class is so deplorably ignorant as to imagine that they are observing *Law and Order* whilst they are ranging the country, forcibly putting a stop to industry, crippling the first movement of every mill and every workshop, driving the workmen from their labour, and preventing the masters from making use of their own

lawful property, – and all this for the avowed purpose of *overa_* _
the Government, and compelling it to change the Constitution; – if,
we say, any class is so deplorably ignorant as to think that acts
like these are justifiable, are honest, are consistent with the existence of Freedom or of Peace; – if they think that the Terror
inspired, the Tyranny exercised, and the immense Danger
incurred, may be excused because the authors of these acts do not
commit wholesale destruction, rapine, and bloodshed; – however
we may commiserate such ignorance, it is necessary for every
friend of his country to exclaim with a voice of earnest warning and
indignant reprehension, that LAW AND ORDER MUST BE
MAINTAINED. . . .

Our conviction is that the real cause of the present Insurrection
is long-continued, wide-spread, gnawing Distress, which we
commiserate with our whole hearts, and which we have most stren-
uously laboured to prevent or to cure: but by the destruction of
Law and Order that Distress will be *immensely aggravated*. . . .

'The Holiday-Insurrection', editorial in *Leeds Mercury*, 20 August
1842.

document 23
The Chartists and the Anti-Corn Law League

*Sheffield was a centre of working-class support for the repeal of the Corn
Laws, but most Chartists were suspicious of the middle-class capitalists who
led the Anti-Corn Law League. In this extract a group of London Chartists
reject overtures from Sheffield for co-operation with the ACLL.*

We are called on to lay aside party strife, and cordially unite with
them, to agitate for a repeal of the Corn-laws. Thereby assuming
that which has no foundation in fact. For our cause, which is the
people's cause, is not the cause of party or faction, but the cause
of the great mass of the industrious classes. . . .

Our object in addressing you is to expose the wickedness and
craft of those who renouncing all principle (except a bad one), are
endeavouring to persuade you to sacrifice your principles on the
altar of expediency, by leaving the people to join a party comprised
of avaricious, grasping money-mongers, great capitalists, and rich
manufacturers.

The quarrel of the factious party we are invited to join is with the landed aristocracy of the country, therefore, let them fight their own battle without our assistance. Seeing they have ever refused to unite with, and assist us in contending for the manly and noble principle of self government, let us remain where we are, and keep the same object in view, and we shall assuredly obtain it.

The Charter, 29 December, 1839.

document 24

Chartism and women

Chartism involved women as well as men as active participants, and there were many local women's groups, like this one from Newcastle. But women's Chartism was hardly a movement for women's liberation. Chartism was seen as a movement for the emancipation of the poor, and was thought of in traditional patriarchal terms.

FELLOW-COUNTRY WOMEN, – We call upon you to join us and help our fathers, husbands, and brothers, to free themselves and us from political, physical, and mental bondage, and urge the following reasons as an answer to our enemies and an inducement to our friends.

We have been told that the province of woman is her home, and that the field of politics should be left to men; this we deny; the nature of things renders it impossible, and the conduct of those who give the advice is at variance with the principles they assert. Is it not true that the interests of our fathers, husbands, and brothers, ought to be ours? If they are oppressed and impoverished, do we not share those evils with them? If so, ought we not to resent the infliction of those wrongs upon them? . . .

For years we have struggled to maintain our homes in comfort, such as our hearts told us should greet our husbands after their fatiguing labours. Year after year have passed away, and even now our wishes have no prospect of being realised, our husbands are over wrought, our houses half furnished, our families ill-fed, and our children uneducated – the fear of want hangs over our heads; the scorn of the rich is pointed towards us; the brand of slavery is on our kindred, and we feel the degradation. We are a despised caste; our oppressors are not content with despising our feelings, but demand the control of our thoughts and wants! – want's bitter

bondage binds us to their feet, we are oppressed becaus
poor − . . .

'Address of the Female Political Union of Newcastle-upon-Tyne to
their Fellow-countrywomen', *Northern Star*, 9 February, 1839.

The new move − education

*Lovett and Collins wrote their tract on Chartism while in Warwick gaol,
1839–40. At the centre of their thesis lay the importance of education, which
in this extract is defined in Owenite terms on to which political conclusions
are grafted.*

In endeavouring to point out the social and political importance
of education, and the necessity for establishing a *better* and more
general system than has hitherto been adopted in this country, it will
be advisable to begin by giving a clear definition of what we mean by
the term '*education*'.

As it applies to *children*, we understand it to imply *all those means*
which are used to develop the various faculties of mind and body,
and so to train them, that the child shall become a healthy, intel-
ligent, moral, and useful member of society.

But in its more extended sense, as it applies *to men and nations*,
it means all those varied circumstances that exercise their influence
on human beings from the cradle to the grave. Hence a man's
parental or scholastic training, his trade or occupation, his social
companions, his pleasures and pursuits, his religion, the institutions, laws, and government of his country, all operate in various
ways to train or educate his physical, mental, and moral powers;
and as all these influences are perfect or defective in character, in character,
so will he be *well or badly educated*. Differences of character will be
found in the same class, according to the modified circumstances
that have operated on each individual; but the *general character* of
each class, community, or nation stands prominently forward,
affording a forcible illustration of the effects of individual, social,
and political *education*. According to *the mental or moral instruction each*
INDIVIDUAL *may receive*, will he be the better able to withstand
social taint and political corruption, and will, by his laudable
example and energy, be advancing the welfare of society, while he
is promoting his own. According *to the intellectual and moral spirit*

which *pervades* SOCIETY, will its individual members be improved; and in proportion as it is ignorant or demoralized, will they be deteriorated by its contact: and *as despotism or freedom prevail in a* NATION, will its subjects be imbued with feelings of liberty, or be drilled into passive slaves.

W. Lovett and J. Collins (**2**), pp. 63–4.

Religious Chartism **document 26**

Chartism in Scotland had a markedly religious tone, especially in its period-ical literature, as the rhythms and phrases of the following passage, no less than its contents, exemplify.

Christian Chartists! ye have now begun to worship God in your own churches. Go on and prosper, and the Almighty will bless you. Let honest, religious, prudent men only be permitted to address you on religious subjects; and let wise teachers be appointed to educate your children, and teach them Christian Chartist doctrines. Instruct, exhort, and console the people; cherish the young; establish the weak; cheer and support the aged; and mildly dispense the ordinances of God to every honest man who asketh. Let baptism and the Lord's Supper be regularly administered, and let the adult participants of the *latter* conduct themselves soberly, righteously, and godly. 'He that putteth his hand to the plough, and looketh back, is not fit for the kingdom of God.' Let us march triumphantly forward on the sacred way that leads to civil and religious liberty, equality, and happiness. Let us press towards the glorious goal of Universal Suffrage, until we reach it; and let Chris-tian Chartism be (what it ought to be) a deep, religious, political feeling, implanted in our minds, by the Eternal, fostered by education, and perfected by circumstances, having benevolence and honesty for its practice, and the happiness of *man* for its object; . . .

'The Christian Chartist Church', *The Chartist Circular*, 29 August, 1840.

O'Connor on Church, Teetotal, Knowledge, and Household Suffrage Chartism

From prison, O'Connor viewed with alarm the various new directions in which Chartism was moving, and he addressed this characteristic letter to his 'children' on the subject. The final paragraph of this extract is a good example of O'Connor's rumbustious brand of sarcasm. In the same issue of the Northern Star *in which this appeared, the editor, William Hill, devoted a long editorial to answering O'Connor point by point, attributing his attitude to his being out of touch whilst in prison.*

I am anxious to see every Chartist a good Christian, a good neighbour, and a good friend. I am desirous of seeing every Chartist sober, industrious, honest, full of knowledge and filling houses; and it is because I believe, in my soul and my conscience, that a hypocritical use of those inestimable blessings will impede, or altogether destroy their possession, that I thus array myself, single-handed, against the quadruple alliance. . . .

My friends, get your Charter, and I will answer for the religion, sobriety, knowledge, and house and a bit of land into the bargain. Upon the other hand, foster your Church and you nurse a viper in your bosom, ready to sting you to death, rather than allow you to thrive to her detriment. . . .

. . . Let them call themselves the Hokey Pokey, New Brummagem, or old Jerusalem, froth and flummerites, and preach Southey and Shelley, and play the Highland bagpipes, as a means of regenerating man, till they are black in the face. . . .

Northern Star, 3 April, 1841.

document 28

The land

When John Marshall, the Leeds millowner, put forward a scheme for allotments for the working classes, O'Connor took the opportunity to address an editorial to his followers pointing out the uselessness of this proposal but the soundness of real settlements on the land. This is an early hint of the direction in which O'Connor's mind was moving, and suggests the practical reasoning behind the 'back to the land' theories of both Chartists and Owenites.

Where are we to find employment for the machinery-displaced labourer, but upon the land! The loud cry of distress that rings through our manufacturing towns arises mainly from the fact, that in the processes of manufacture, male adult labour has been almost entirely superseded, either by the *cheaper* labour of adult females, infantile 'hands', or inanimate machinery. Of WORK there is enough! The mills and other manufacturing establishments turn out plenty of manufactured goods! But those goods are mostly machine-made. Adult labour is not now in request in their production. Vast numbers of able-bodied labourers are without employment, even when our manufactories are running extra hours; and these in their endeavour to procure the means of existence at all, necessarily pull down the wages of those of their brethren who are fortunate enough to procure employment, by offering their services at a less and still less rate of remuneration. And this process is constantly going on! More machinery is constantly being set up; and machines still further simplifying the manufacturing processes, and still further dispensing with animate attendance, are daily being introduced. . . . Adult labour is being *driven* out of the manufacturing labour-market. For a while the superseded ones live on the earnings of their wives or their 'little ones'; then the parish is appealed to; the *man* becomes broken-spirited and *pauperized*; squalid misery, abject wretchedness, and utter destitution is the consequence! and enough of this meets the eye at every turn. . . .

The position we should wish man to occupy on THE LAND, is one of independence! To be there his own master! To have sufficient of surface in his occupation to occupy his labour hours, and to return him an adequate LIVING. To so occupy, that every improvement he made should be mainly his own, so that he might have every inducement to make improvements. In fine, we wish, in having the people allocated on THE LAND, to form a *natural market* for labour, which, in its operation, shall so affect the artificial market, as to *cause* the producer in the latter to have sufficient wherewith to feed, clothe, shelter, and well-educate himself. . . .

'The Land! The only means of salvation for the starving workers', editorial *Northern Star*, 14 January, 1843.

document 29

O'Connorville

This description of the scene at an 'open day' at the Chartist Land Company's first estate at Heronsgate, near Rickmansworth, Hertfordshire (renamed O'Connorville), exemplifies the enthusiasm and carnival-like atmosphere which Chartist occasions could generate.

On arriving at O'Connorville, at twelve o'clock, we found a vast number of persons had preceded us by other routes; the 'Ordnance', nevertheless, greeted this new accession of strength, by a roar of thunder from its 'Iron throat'. We had ocular demonstration that this demonstration was no mere metropolitan pleasure excursion, but 'A National Jubilee', in favour of the 'Universal Rights' of man, each county appearing to have at least a fair share of representatives present; even from Yorkshire and Lancashire in the north; and from Exeter and Plymouth in the West. . . .

On entering the gates, the band played 'The Chartist Land March'. . . . The first object that met our view, was a huge tricoloured banner floating, high above an immense chestnut tree, bearing the inscription, 'O'Connorville'; and secondly, Rebecca, the Chartist Cow, like the Sacred Cows of old, clothed in her vesture of tri-colour, rendered holy by the popular voice, which is the voice of God; next, the immense Dancing Booth, erected for the accommodation of our Chartist friends, attracting the attention of everyone. The remaining booths, for refreshment and amusement, were also of a very elegant character. Several 'Wandering Minstrels' attended, and earned the patronage of the visitors by singing 'The People's First Estate'. . . .

Northern Star, 22 August, 1846.

document 30

Gammage on O'Connor

Gammage's History *is biased against O'Connor, but is nevertheless valuable for its verbal portraits of the leaders, drawn from life. This picture of O'Connor shows a grudging recognition of his qualities as a leader. Note the typically nineteenth-century reference to phrenology, to which Gammage was attracted.*

Upwards of six feet in height, stout and athletic, and in spite of his opinions invested with a sort of aristrocratic bearing, the sight of his person was calculated to inspire the masses with a solemn awe. So true is it that despite the march of civilisation, and the increase of respect for mental superiority, men are generally impressed with a veneration for superior physical power. O'Connor's short neck – so short as to be imperceptible to the beholder, was the only defect in his physical appearance, and even this, so far from conveying an unfavourable impression, rather enhanced than detracted from the idea which the public entertained of the great strength of his iron frame.

O'Connor however did not depend alone upon physical strength for the involuntary respect in which he was held by the multitude. His broad massive forehead, very full in those parts where phrenologists place the organs of perception, though considerably deficient in the faculties of reflection, bore evidence, in spite of these defects, of great intellectual force. To assert that he possessed a mind solid and steady were to say too much, no man with an equal amount of intellect was ever more erratic. Had the solidity of his judgment been equal to his quickness of perception he would intellectually have been a great man, but this essential quality of greatness he lacked, hence his life presents a series of mistakes and contradictions, which, as men reflected more lowered him in their estimation. No man in the movement was so certain of popularity as O'Connor. No man was so certain to lose it after its attainment. It was not till he proceeded to speak that the full effect of his influence was felt. This however depended upon circumstances. With an indoor assembly Vincent was by far his superior. Out of doors O'Connor was the almost universal idol, for the thunder of his voice would reach the ears of the most careless, and put to silence the most noisy of his audience.

R. G. Gammage, (**7**), p. 45.

document 31

Place on the 'Northern Star'

Francis Place was no admirer of Feargus O'Connor, popular demagogy, or socialist ideas, as the following extract (written in 1843) makes clear, and through his papers Place has determined the bias of much writing on the subject since his day. Nevertheless, this passage remains an acute analysis of the way in which the Northern Star, *for better or worse, operated within the Chartist movement, inspiring hopeless optimism among both leaders and followers.*

The Northern Star was carried on with remarkable vigour, without regard to honour or honesty or truth in any respect which at the moment was in the opinion of the proprietor and editor likely to increase the absurd and mischievous popularity of O'Connor and the sale of the paper. . . .

The Editor of the Northern Star collected accounts of political meetings from all parts, in London and some other large towns people were paid to collect this kind of information, and in every place the active radical reformers being desirous of notice were willing to furnish accounts, and every meeting if even only half a dozen persons were present were represented as meetings at particular places and the reader was led to conclude that they were meetings of considerable numbers of inhabitants of the place. Meetings which were attended by many persons were reported at length and the smaller meetings in longer or shorter paragraphs, the reports of each of the large meetings filling many columns and the small meetings being many in number occupying one or more whole pages. Thus the paper became the medium of communication between all radical reformers, its sale continued to increase rapidly, and that of all the other radical papers fell. . . .

O'Brien wrote long and well adapted papers to the notions which had been carefully instilled into each of the vast number of working men who took an interest in public matters. . . . They were grossly misled and sadly abused, but the writings of O'Brien tended to increase the sale of the paper, helped to make O'Connor a great man in his own conceit, enabled him to pay Hill and O'Brien money enough to induce them to go on vigorously, and by the constant application of the same sentiments satisfy themselves that the commencement of the change they had predicted was near at hand, and led to the assurances each of these men soon afterwards gave the people that, the whole of the six points for which they had contended would be enacted by the Parliament on a day they named, . . . From their proceedings subsequent to the time now treated of no doubt can be entertained that these men fully expected to see all that they had promised accomplished.

Francis Place, '*Historical Narrative, 1838.* British Library, Add. Mss 27,820, pp. 154–5.

..y on Chartist leadership

In the mid-1840s, Harney came to know Engels through the Northern Star *office in Leeds, beginning a fruitful relationship which stimulated Harney's interest in European affairs and the development of his socialist thought. In this letter, Harney's realism, which had been growing since 1840, is in contrast to Engels' still inexperienced youthful enthusiasm. Harney's assessment of the prospects for revolution, and his appraisal of O'Connor's worth, offer points of importance for the historian of Chartism to consider.*

Your speculations as to the speedy coming of a revolution in England I doubt. Revolutionary changes in Germany I think certain and likely to come soon. Such changes are not less certain in France and likely to ensue soon after the death of that old scoundrel Louis-Philippe, but I confess I cannot see the likelihood of such changes in England at least until England is moved from *without* as well as within. Your prediction that we will get the Charter in the course of the present year, and the abolition of private property within three years will certainly not be realized; – indeed as regards the latter, although it may and I hope will come, it is my belief that neither you nor I will see it. As to what O'C[onnor] has been saying lately about "physical force," I think nothing of it. The English people will not adopt [Thomas] Cooper's slavish notions about peace and non-resistance but neither would they *act* upon the opposite doctrine. They applaud it at public meetings, but that is all. Notwithstanding all the talk in 1839 about 'arming,' the people did not arm, and they will not arm. A long immunity from the presence of war in their own country and the long suspension of the militia has created a general distaste for arms, which year by year is becoming more extensive and more intense. The *body* of the English people, without becoming a slavish people, are becoming an eminently pacific people. . . . To attempt a 'physical-force' agitation at the present time would be productive of no good but on the contrary of some evil – the evil of exciting suspicion against the agitators. I do not suppose that the great changes which will come in this country will come altogether without violence, but organized combats such as we may look for in France, Germany, Italy and Spain, cannot take place in this country. To organize, to conspire a revolution in this country would be a vain and foolish project and the men who with their eyes open could take part in so absurd an attempt would be worse than foolish, would be highly culpable.

I must next notice what you say about my '*leadership*'. First let me remark that you are too hard upon O'Connor. . . . I must do O'C. the justice to say that he never interferes with what I write in the paper nor does he know what I write until he sees the paper. You have thought proper in the letter I am now commenting on to credit me with all the revolutionary virtues. You say I am 'international', 'revolutionary', 'energetical', 'proletarian', 'more of a Frenchman than an Englishman', 'Atheistical, Republican and Communist'. I am too old a soldier to blush at this accumulation of virtues credited to my account, but supposing it to be even as you say, it does not follow that I am qualified for 'leadership'. A popular chief should be possessed of a magnificent bodily appearance, an iron frame, eloquence, or at least a ready fluency of tongue. I have none of these. O'C. has them all – at least in degree. A popular leader should possess great animal courage, contempt of pain and death, and be not altogether ignorant of arms and military science. No chief or leader that has hitherto appeared in the English movement has these qualifications. . . . In these qualifications I am decidedly deficient. I know nothing of arms, have no stomach for fighting, and would rather die after some other fashion than by bullet or rope. From a knowledge of myself and all the men who live, and do figure in the Chartist movement, I am convinced that even in this respect, was O'C. thrown overboard, we might go further and fare worse. . . .

G. J. Harney to F. Engels, 30 March 1846, in F. G. and R.M. Black, (**12**) pp. 239–42.

document 33

Chartist continuity in Halifax, 1848

Ben Wilson's recollections here serve to remind us that, despite the collapse of the mass movement and the dwindling membership of the NCA, there was radical continuity throughout the 1840s, based on the Northern Star. *Wilson also admits, though, the dependence of the mass movement on the price of bread.*

In this year flour was very dear, reaching the price of 5s. per stone, whilst trade was also very bad. This was the time to make politicians, as the easiest way to get to an Englishman's brains is through his stomach. It was said by its enemies that Chartism was dead and buried and would never rise again, but they were doomed to disappointment. It was true there had been no meetings or processions, nor had the agitation reached the height it attained in 1839, but it was going on. Amongst combers, handloom weavers, and others politics was the chief topic. The *Northern Star* was their principal paper, and it was a common practice, particularly in villages, to meet at friends' houses to read the paper and talk over political matters. We met at a friend's at Skircoat Green, but occasionally I went to a friend's house at Cinderhills, where there was sure to be a good many friends. We were only waiting for the time to come again.

Benjamin Wilson, (**47d**), p. 206.

document 34

The springtime of the peoples, 1848

Harney's great interest in foreign affairs, and his excitement at the continental revolutions of 1848, is vividly revealed in this call to action, which, although never actually prosecuted, must have come close to incitement to treason. The European revolutions seemed to provide that external stimulus which he had looked for in 1846 [**doc. 32**].

Glory to the Proletarians of Paris, they have saved the Republic!

The work goes bravely on. Germany is revolutionised from end to end. Princes are flying, thrones are perishing. Everywhere the oppressors of nations yield, or are overthrown. 'Reform or Revolution' is now the order of the day.

How long, Men of Great Britain and Ireland, how long will you carry the damning stigma of being the only people in Europe who dare not will their freedom?

Patience! the hour is nigh! From the hill-tops of Lancashire, from the voices of hundreds of thousands has ascended to Heaven the oath of union, and the rallying cry of conflict. Englishmen and Irishmen have sworn to have THE CHARTER AND REPEAL, or VIVE LA REPUBLIQUE!

'The Paris Proletarians', editorial in the *Northern Star*, 25 March, 1848.

document 35
The Kennington Common meeting, 10 April 1848

With the Queen safely on the Isle of Wight, the Prime Minister took excessive precautions to prevent a disturbance when the Chartists gathered to march on Parliament with their third petition, and by early afternoon on 10 April he was able to send this gratifying report to Her Majesty.

Lord John Russell presents his humble duty to your Majesty, and has the honour to state that the Kennington Common Meeting has proved a complete failure.

About 12,000 or 15,000 persons met in good order. Feargus O'Connor, upon arriving upon the ground in a car, was ordered by Mr Mayne [the Commissioner of Police – ed.] to come and speak to him. He immediately left the car and came, looking pale and frightened, to Mr Mayne. Upon being told that the meeting would not be prevented, but that no procession would be allowed to pass the bridges, he expressed the utmost thanks, and begged to shake Mr Mayne by the hand. He then addressed the crowd, advising them to disperse, and after rebuking them for their folly he went off in a cab to the Home Office, where he repeated to Sir George Grey [the Home Secretary – ed.] his thanks, his fears, and his assurances that the crowd should disperse quietly. Sir George Grey said he had done very rightly, but that the force at the bridges should not be diminished.

Mr F. O'Connor – 'Not a man should be taken away. The Government have been quite right. I told the Convention that if they had been the Government they never would have allowed such a meeting.'

The last account gave the numbers as about 5,000 rapidly dispersing.

The mob was in good humour, and any mischief that now takes place will be the act of individuals; but it is to be hoped the preparations made will daunt those wicked but not brave men.

The accounts from the country are good. Scotland is quiet. At Manchester, however, the Chartists are armed, and have bad designs.

A quiet termination of the present ferment will greatly raise us in foreign countries.

Lord John Russell trusts your Majesty has profited by the sea air.

Lord John Russell to Queen Victoria, 2 p.m. 10 April 1848, in
A. C. Benson and Viscount Esher, eds, *The Letters of Queen Victoria*,
3 vols, London, 1908, II, pp. 168–9.

document 36

The London revolution, 1848

*Chartist unrest continued throughout the spring and summer of 1848, though
the revolutionaries were only a small minority, led on by government spies.
Thomas Frost's account is one of the most vivid and detailed of the sources
describing the activities from within the Chartist movement. Continental
revolutionary tactics are clearly evident.*

On the evening of the 15th of August, which was finally fixed for
the outbreak, a number of men assembled at a public-house called
the Orange Tree, in Orange Street, Bloomsbury, and were in
feverish expectation of the signal, when an inspector of police
appeared at the door of the room in which they were seated, with
a drawn cutlass in his right hand, and a cocked pistol in his left.
Behind him those seated opposite the door could see a dozen
constables, all similarly armed. There was a movement among the
party as he entered, indicative of meditated resistance or escape;
but it was checked by the threat to shoot down the first who
resisted, or attempted to leave the room.

Commanding each in his turn to stand up, the inspector then
searched them, and afterwards the room. A sword was found under
the coat of one, and the head of a pike, made to screw into a socket,
under that of another. One had a pair of pistols in his pocket, and
a fourth was provided with a rusty bayonet, fastened to the end
of a stick. Some were without other weapons than shoemakers'
knives. A pike, which no one would own, was found under a bench
upon which several of the men had been sitting. All of the party
were taken into custody, and marched off to the nearest police-
station. . . .

While these arrests were being made, about 150 men were
assembled on the Seven Dials – standing in groups at the street
corners, or before the bars of the public-houses. Just after the
arrests at the Orange Tree, a man approached a group at the
corner of Great St Andrew Street, and spoke a few hurried words
in a low voice to a labourer, who, with a pickaxe in his hand, was
directing the attention of his companions to a loose stone in the

pavement of the roadway. Almost at the same moment a body of police made their appearance, but apparently without other intention than being in readiness for something.

The man moved quickly from one group to another, and as he left each the men composing it separated, some walking quietly away, and others entering the public-houses at the corner of the streets to communicate what they had heard to those assembled inside. In this manner the number of men assembled on the Dials was reduced in a few minutes to about a tenth of those who had been found there – a result which was attributed by the authorities to the appearance of the police, but was really due to the warning so promptly conveyed to the men.

I have since been informed that the flag of the revolt was to have been first unfurled at this spot, upon which barricades were to have been erected – the beginning of a series to have been extended on every side from the centre – until the insurgents were able to hem in the seat of the Court and the Government. . . .

Thomas Frost, (**44**) pp. 163–5.

document 37

Compromise

With moderation and a sense of realism growing after 1848, the editorial policy of the Northern Star *became markedly less antagonistic to middle-class radicals. In this article the terms of a working alliance with the National Parliamentary and Financial Reform Association are set out. This editorial may have been written by O'Connor himself or by G. A. Fleming, sub-editor and later editor of the paper, but probably not by Harney who was still the nominal editor in 1849.*

. . . The middle and working classes have joined hands, without reserve or dissimulation. The one party says they cannot go further at present – the other, that they will accompany them as far as they go, but they do not mean to stop there. The ancient and honoured motto is not even in abeyance. We still exclaim, 'The Charter and No Surrender!' but, taught by dear-bought past experience, we have varied the mode of operation by which it is to be attained.

This junction between the middle and working classes is the one great event of the past year upon which we have to congratulate ourselves and our readers. The prospect of ultimate success brightens upon us. The day of political redemption draws nigh. Against the combined forces of the producers and distributors of wealth, the idle drones and usurious monopolists of society cannot stand. . . .

'Our Anniversary', editorial in the *Northern Star*, 17 November, 1849.

'The New World' document 38

Ernest Jones wrote the long poem from which this passage is extracted while in prison (1848–50), partly in his own blood, and he published it as the first article in his Notes to the People *(1851). The theme is the class struggle, and here he is treating the middle-class betrayal of 1832. The poem illustrates Jones's considerable powers as a poet.*

Again the murmuring populace ferment:
This time the TRADERS stir the discontent.
As yet their titled rivals share the spoil:
'To us – to us alone – the mines of toil!
'*If burdens crush ye, and if bread is high,*
'*The landlords – the landlords are to blame!*' they cry.
'Their vile monopolies, that feudal wreck!
'Restrict our trade, and thus your labour check.'

The suffering mass, unreasoning in their grief,
Grasp at each straw that promises relief;
They hear the dangerous half-truth, – pause, and trust, –
And an old system tumbles in the dust.
Then burst anew the deeply-rankling hate: –
The smiling traders watch their game, and wait.
Down sinks the noble! – down the scutcheons fall!
Death strikes the castle – ruin wraps the hall!
Stout labour sweeps the gilded dross away,
And holds its saturnalia of – a day!

The renovated sacrifice is o'er:
The People hope their paradise once more.
From town to town resounds the enlivening cheer –
The danger past – the middle class appear.

Still flood the masses – but they lull the storm:
'Disarm! – go home! – and wait – *while* we *reform*!
'To us your hopes and griefs alike are known.
'And we will guard your interests – as our own!'

Time passes – and the wrongs are unredressed –
Still crushed by burdens – still by taxes pressed –
Still bread is high – and still are wages scant –
Still that the rich may waste, the poor may want.
True 'tis no more the nobles' lazy pride, –
But heavier still the bloated burghers ride.
The name is altered – lives the substance still, –
And what escaped the mansion meets the mill.
Wondering, they wake to find, once more betrayed,
'Tis but a change of tyrants they have made.
Again the whispers float, the murmurs rise,
And angry plaints are met with ready lies:
'The wrongs so many centuries saw endure,
'A few short months of change can hardly cure.'
And 'give us time!' – and 'give us time!' they cried:
Another generation starved and died.

'The New World', *Notes to the People*, I, p. 10 (3 May, 1851).

document 39

Tribute to a veteran Chartist

This obituary notice is typical of the many which appeared in radical papers
of the later nineteenth century. The writer conveys the usual sentiments that
gradual reform was 'sensible' but that the Chartists were nonetheless men to
be proud of.

JOHN SNOWDEN. – With sadness and grief must one who knew
him well record here the death of the veteran Chartist and
Reformer, John Snowden, of Halifax. Sixty-two years of life were
his, forty-six of them years of active political warfare, with its
episodes intertwined with historic issues. His youth was inspired
by the fellowship of once famous, now vanished leaders, from
whom he caught that enthusiasm which made him subserve everything to the one great end of helping on the day of the people. John
Snowden was nothing if not a politician; and he worked for the

Charter with might and main while Chartism was a possible force to be reckoned with in this country. The cause flickered feebly in 1842, and finally flared out in 1848; and John Snowden then sensibly espoused the cause of gradual reform, working steadfastly at the task nearest hand, training his brain the while with home study of history and of political principles; debating and acquiring a rugged eloquence of no copyist type, and a skill of speech welcomed by ears of toilers, because it spake through sympathy of touch with horny hand at workshop and loom, a sympathy cemented, too, by fellowship in poverty. Then we find John Snowden as a delegate to Reform Conferences, one after another. . . . In 1866, Hyde Park railings fall with the Yorkshire Radical's heel set thereon; and then come peacefuller times, with the favour of fellow-burgesses placing him for nine years on the School Board of the borough – once, too, at the head of the poll. Liberal meeting and demonstration were never without his presence; and we find him standing out bravely, too, for Northampton's constitutional right. The oft-expressed wish of his life was to live to see the assimilation of the county with the borough suffrage; but alas! much to his and our regret, the outworn energies have had to succumb, and the dim eyes to close, with two million brethren still waiting for the Franchise. – J. H. SIMPSON.

National Reformer, 7 September, 1884.

document 40

The Tory view of Chartism in fiction

Reflecting on a lifetime of agitation, the veteran Owenite and Chartist, G. J. Holyoake, clearly distinguished between those views which attributed unrest to material hardship (Tory), and those which attributed it to the denial of political rights (Radical). For Holyoake, not only were friends of the working classes like Owen, Oastler and Stephens all Tories, but even the Christian Socialist Charles Kingsley and the Positivist George Eliot had not truly appreciated the political significance of Chartism as a Radical movement. The question remains, however, whether Chartism was truly Radical in this sense.

There is a noble sympathy with labour, and there are passages which should always be read with honour in 'Alton Locke'. But the book is written in derision of Chartism and Liberal politics. . . .
   . . . George Eliot had greater power of penetrating into character

than Kingsley, but she made the same mistake in Felix Holt that Kingsley made in Alton Locke. Felix Holt is a revolutionist from indignation. His social insurgency is based on resentment at injustice. Very noble is that form of dissatisfaction, but political independence is not his inspiration. Freedom, equality of public rights, are not in his mind. His disquiet is not owing to the political inability of his fellows to control their own fortunes. Content comes to Felix when the compassion of others ameliorates or extinguishes the social evils from which his fellows suffer. He is the Chartist of Positivism without a throb of indignation at political subjection. That may be Positivism, but it is not Radicalism.

Felix Holt discloses his character in his remark that 'the Radical question was how to give every man a man's share in life. But I think that is to expect voting to do more towards it than I do.' . . . Holt's depreciation of the power of voting was the argument of the benevolent but beguiling Tory. It was part of the Carlylean contempt for a ten-thousandth part of a voice in the 'national palava'. This meant distrust, not only of the suffrage, but of Parliament itself. When both are gone, despotism becomes supreme. When Felix Holt talked so, he ceased to be a Radical – if ever he was one.

G. J. Holyoake, *Bygones Worth Remembering*, 2 vols, 1905, I, pp. 90–2.

document 41

Political apathy in 1870

In this entirely personal view of changes in working-class political consciousness since the days of Chartism, Thomas Cooper begs a central question about the nature of the British working-class movement in the nineteenth century. Is he exaggerating the political consciousness of the Chartists, or overestimating the extent to which increasing material comforts had depoliticised the working classes after 1850?

In our old Chartist time, it is true, Lancashire working men were in rags by thousands; and many of them often lacked food. But their intelligence was demonstrated wherever you went. You would see them in groups discussing the great doctrine of political justice – that every grown-up, sane man ought to have a vote in the election of the men who were to make the laws by which he was to be governed; or they were in earnest dispute respecting the teach-

131

ings of Socialism. *Now*, you will see no such groups in Lancashire. But you will hear well-dressed working men talking, as they walk with their hands in their pockets, of 'Co-ops' (Co-operative Stores), and their shares in them, or in building societies. And you will see others, like idiots, leading small greyhound dogs, covered with cloth, in a string! They are about to race, and they are betting money as they go! And yonder comes another clamorous dozen of men, cursing and swearing and betting upon a few pigeons they are about to let fly! As for their betting on horses – like their masters! – it is a perfect madness.

Except in Manchester and Liverpool – where, of course, intelligence is to be found, if it be found anywhere in England, – I gathered no large audiences in Lancashire. Working men had ceased to think and wanted to hear no thoughtful talk; at least, it was so with the greater number of them. To one who has striven hard, the greater part of his life, to instruct and elevate them, and who has suffered and borne imprisonment for them, all this was more painful than I care to tell.

Thomas Cooper, (**43**), pp. 393–4.

A final verdict

document 42

Ramsden Balmforth, son of a Huddersfield Chartist handloom weaver, and brought up in a home filled with Chartist and Owenite memories, gave his final verdict on Chartism in 1900. His views, which probably reflect those of his father (who did not die till 1904), raise a number of important issues for consideration in any assessment of the importance of Chartism and the reasons for its failure. The blame placed on O'Connor typifies the attitude of most of Chartism's first historians. Balmforth's views may also have been shaped by his involvement in the Ethical Movement and the Independent Labour Party.

The Chartist movement was one to which all social and political reformers look back with a certain amount of pride, mingled with a great amount of sadness. Pride, because it was a movement inspired by great ideals; because it called forth a spirit of devotion and self-sacrifice which is rare in public movements, and caught up on its 'moral force' side some of the finest and most thoughtful working-men of the time. Sadness, because its ideals were either shattered, or passed on, by the natural process of evolution, into other movements and other parties; because its spirit of devotion and self-sacrifice was broken by brutal persecution and imprisonment; and because its 'moral force' was largely neutralised, and its adherents deluded and misled, by one or two inordinately vain and self-seeking agitators.

. . . Of these, perhaps the most culpable was Feargus O'Connor. O'Connor was the editor and chief proprietor of the 'Northern Star', the principal working-class newspaper of the time, and, through its pages, wielded great influence. Possessing lungs of brass and a voice like a trumpet, he was the most effective outdoor orator of his time, and the idol of the immense assemblages which were often brought together in those days. Unfortunately, both for the movement and for himself, he was a man of unbounded conceit and egotism, extremely jealous of precedence, and regarding himself as a sort of uncrowned king of the working classes . . . But it would be a great mistake to suppose that the Chartist movement was really fruitless. No movement of its magnitude and intensity can be fruitless. It may have looked too much to outward means, and too little to inward and spiritual reform; but it was an excellent means of political education for the working classes.

Ramsden Balmforth, *Some Social and Political Pioneers of the Nineteenth Century*, London, 1900, pp. 187, 189, 196.

Chronology

1835

17 September	Marylebone Radical Association founded by O'Connor
Autumn	Local Radical Associations founded
December	O'Connor's lecture tour of the North

1836

26 June	London Working Men's Association founded
August	National Radical Association of Scotland founded

1837

24 January	LWMA petition drafted, embodying the Six Points
January	East London Democratic Association founded
	Poor Law Commissioners move North
28 February	First LWMA public meeting
March	LWMA missionary activity begins
	Worsening of economic situation
17 March	Central National Association founded
15 May	Poor Law meeting on Hartshead Moor, West Riding
23 May	Birmingham Political Union revived
31 May &	Statement of the Six Points issued by meeting of
7 June	six LWMA members and six Radical MPs
July	General election – defeat of Radical MPs
18 November	*Northern Star* published in Leeds, ed. William Hill

1838

April	Great Northern Union formed in Leeds
May	LDA reconstituted in opposition to LWMA
8 May	The People's Charter published
14 May	BPU adopts National Petition
21 May	Glasgow Green meeting adopts Petition and Charter

6 August	Meeting at Holloway Head, Birmingham marks the beginning of Chartism in England
17 September	Meeting in Palace Yard, Westminster
24 September	Kersal Moor meeting to elect Lancashire delegates
September	Northern Political Union revived in Newcastle
15 October	Hartshead Moor (Peep Green) meeting
8 December	Meeting on Calton Hill, Edinburgh, declares for 'moral force'
27 December	J. R. Stephens the first Chartist to be arrested

1839

27 January	*Charter* newspaper published in London
4 February	General Convention meets in London
20 March	Anti-Corn Law League founded
21 March	John Frost dismissed from magistracy
4 April	C. J. Napier appointed to command in the North
13 April	*Democrat* published in London (Harney)
30 April	Rioting begins in Llanidloes
7 May	Petition ready; 'Bedchamber crisis'
13 May	Convention moves to Birmingham
20 May	Mass meeting on Newcastle Town Moor
21 May	Mass meeting on Peep Green
25 May	Mass meeting on Kersal Moor
May	Rebecca Riots begin in Wales
14 June	Petition presented by Attwood and Fielden, with 1,280,000 signatures
July	Bull Ring riots in Birmingham
5 July	Convention agrees resolutions denouncing police
6 July	Lovett and Collins arrested
10 July	Convention returns to London
12 July	Charter rejected by 235 to 46
17 July	Convention calls for a 'Sacred Month'
24 July	Rural Police Bill introduced in Parliament
6 August	'Sacred Month' called off and Convention prorogued
15 August	Universal Suffrage Central Committee for Scotland elected
28 September	*Chartist Circular* published in Glasgow
4 November	Newport rising
10 December	Special Commission meets to hear cases against Frost etc.

1840

11–12 January	Attempted rising in Sheffield led by Holberry
26–27 January	Attempted rising in Bradford led by Peddie
February– March	Chartist trials
April	Metropolitan Charter Union founded by Hetherington
June	Arthur O'Neill appointed full-time missionary in Lanarkshire; spread of Chartist Churches
20 July	National Charter Association founded in Manchester
24 July	Lovett and Collins released; *Chartism* published

1841

23 January	*English Chartist Circular* published
April	National Association founded by Lovett
August	General election – Conservative victory led by Peel
30 August	O'Connor released
September– October	NCA takes up idea of a new Petition

1842

January	Complete Suffrage Union founded in Birmingham
8 March	O'Connor's Manchester lecture broken up by Irish mob
5 April	CSU conference in Birmingham
12 April	National Convention meets in London NCA claims about 400 localities and 50,000 members
21 April	CSU petition rejected by 226 to 67
2 May	Chartist petition, with 3,317,752 signatures, presented by T. S. Duncombe; rejected by 287 to 49
August– September	Industrial unrest
5 August	Strike begins in Stalybridge
12 August	Conference of trades delegates in Manchester resolves to remain on strike until the Charter is the law of the land
16 August	Commemoration of 'Peterloo' Plug Riots spread to Yorkshire

20 August	Manchester Trades recommend return to work
October	Chartist trials begin
	Recovery of trade
27 December	CSU – Chartist conference in Birmingham – victory for Chartists

1843

March	Lancaster trials of O'Connor etc.
August	Joshua Hobson becomes editor of *Northern Star*
5 September	NCA Convention meets in Birmingham to re-organise NCA; Land Question taken up
October	Harney becomes sub-editor of *Northern Star*

1844

April	NCA Convention in Manchester
5 August	Cobden and O'Connor debate the corn laws at Northampton
30 November	*Northern Star* published in London

1845

March	National Association of United Trades for the Protection of Labour founded
21 April	NCA Convention in London; Chartist Land Co-operative Society approved
22 September	Fraternal Democrats founded
30 October	Harney becomes editor of *Northern Star*
8 December	Manchester conference agrees to the Land Plan

1846

February	Rising in Cracow
March	Heronsgate (O'Connorville) acquired; first ballot announced
26 June	Act passed to repeal the corn laws
October	Lowbands bought
26 December	National Land and Labour Bank established

1847

1 May	O'Connorville opened
June	Snig's End and Minster Lovell (Charterville) acquired
July	General election – Whig minority government led by Lord John Russell
	O'Connor elected for Nottingham

August	Lowbands opened; conference there on Land Plan
	Commercial crisis begins

1848
24 February	Revolution in France
6 March	Income tax demonstration in Trafalgar Square
	Riots in London and Glasgow
7 March	Riots in Manchester
13 March	Meeting on Kennington Common, London
22 March	People's Charter Union founded
4 April	Convention meets
7 April	Security Bill proposed in Parliament
10 April	Chartist demonstration on Kennington Common
	Petition delivered to Parliament by O'Connor
11, 14 April	Convention resolves on further actions
13 April	Petition ridiculed in House of Commons
24 April	People's League founded at National Hall
1 May	National Assembly meets
13 May	National Assembly dissolves after electing a
	Provisional Executive
28 May	Riots in Bradford
29 May	Beginning of meetings and disturbances in
	London
4 June	Riots in London
6 June	Arrest of Ernest Jones in Manchester
12 June	Day of Protest
June	Snig's End and Minster Lovell opened
July	Irish rising aborted by arrests of leaders
15 August	Planned uprising in Britain

1849
29 January	National Parliamentary and Financial Reform
	Association founded
June	*Democratic Review* published (Harney)
July	Great Dodford opened
October	Fraternal Democrats reorganised
19 December	National Reform League programme announced

1850
22 June	*Red Republican* published (Harney)
10 July	Ernest Jones released
August	Harney leaves *Northern Star*

| 6 October | National Charter and Social Reform Union projected |
| December | NCA Executive elections |

1851

31 March	NCA Convention adopts social democratic policy and agrees to differ on collaboration with moderate reformers
3 May	*Notes to the People* published (Jones)
August	Act passed for winding up the Land Company
December	NCA Executive elections – Harney and Jones individually break with NCA

1852

13 January	O'Connor loses control of *Northern Star*
13 March	Last issue of *Northern Star*
1 May	*People's Paper* published (Jones)
8 May	*Star of Freedom* published (Harney)
17 May	Jones calls Chartist conference at Manchester
June	O'Connor declared insane
July	General election – Jones contests Halifax

1854

| March | Crimean War begins |
| October | First part of Gammage's *History* published |

1855

| 30 August | Death of O'Connor |

1856

| 12 July | Return of Frost from exile |

1858

| 8 February | Chartist Conference adopts Jones's motion for co-operation with moderate Radicals |

Bibliography

A complete bibliography of Chartism fills a whole book, namely
J. F. C. Harrison and D. Thompson, *Bibliography of the Chartist
Movement, 1837–1976* (Harvester Press, 1978). There is a select
bibliography in D. Jones, *Chartism and the Chartists* (**38**), and the
footnotes in many of the other items listed below will lead the
interested reader to further books and articles. A guide to
additional background reading will be found in companion
volumes to this Seminar Study by D. G. Wright (**24**) and myself
(**23**). Bibliographies may be kept up-to-date by reference to the
annual lists published in the *Bulletin of the Society for the Study of
Labour History*.

UNPUBLISHED SOURCES
The principal collections are in the British Library (Bloomsbury),
which houses the Francis Place manuscript and newspaper collections, and the records of the London Working Men's Association;
and the Home Office files at the Public Record Office (Kew),
especially the papers referring to disturbances in HO 40, 41 and
45. Most large provincial libraries and county record offices also
have materials of relevance, especially for the local historian.

NEWSPAPERS
There is no convenient collection of all the relevant Chartist newspapers and periodicals, but individual locations can be traced in
The Warwick Guide to British Labour Periodicals compiled by R.
Harrison, G. B. Woolven, and R. Duncan (Harvester, 1977). A
number of these papers have been reprinted, and the major ones
are listed in D. Jones (**38**), the most important being the *Northern
Star* which is available on microfilm. The local historian should
also remember to consult his own local or county newspapers for
the period.

PRINTED SOURCES
1   G. Howell, *A History of the Working Men's Association from 1836*

to 1850 (1900), new edition introduced by D. J. Rowe (Frank Graham, 1970)

2   W. Lovett and J. Collins, *Chartism. A New Organisation for the People* (1840), new edition introduced by A. Briggs (Leicester University Press, 1970)

3   W. Napier *The Life and Opinions of General Sir Charles James Napier*, 4 vols (J. Murray, 1857) – mainly extracts from Napier's letters and journal: see especially vol. II, Epoch 12.

4   C. Godfrey and J. Epstein, 'Notes on sources. HO 20/10. Interviews of Chartist prisoners 1840–41', *Bulletin of the Society for the Study of Labour History* xxxiv (Spring 1977) – contains facsimile reprints of two reports similar to **doc. 14**

5   F. Engels, *The Condition of the Working Class in England* (1845), translated and edited by W. O. Henderson and W. H. Challoner (Blackwell, 1971)

6   F. Peel, *The Risings of the Luddites, Chartists and Plug-Drawers* (1880), new edition with an introduction by E. P. Thompson (Cass, 1968)

7   R. G. Gammage, *History of the Chartist Movement 1837–1854* (1854), second edition 1894, reprinted with an introduction by J. Saville (Kelley, 1969). This is a critical edition; there is also a straight reprint published by Merlin (1969).

EDITED COLLECTIONS OF SOURCES

8   G. D. H. Cole and A. W. Filson, *British Working Class Movements, 1789–1875* (Macmillan, 1951)

9   P. Hollis, *Class and Conflict in Nineteenth-Century England, 1815–1850* (Routledge & Kegan Paul, 1973)

9a   F. C. Mather, *Chartism and Society: an anthology of documents* (Bell & Hyman, 1980)

10   D. Thompson, *The Early Chartists* (Macmillan, 1971)

10a R. Brown and C. Daniels, *The Chartists* (Macmillan, 1984)

11   Y. V. Kovalev, *An Anthology of Chartist Literature* (Moscow, 1956)

12   F. G. and R. M. Black, *The Harney Papers* (Assen, 1969)

Reference should also be made to the *Annual Register, Hansard,* and the *British Sessional Papers* of the two Houses of Parliament

THE NEW SOCIETY

13   H. C. Darby, ed., *A New Historical Geography of England*

(Cambridge University Press, 1973) of which the second part, *After 1600*, was published separately (1976)

14 W. W. Rostow, *The British Economy in the Nineteenth Century* (Oxford University Press, 1948)

15 J. F. C. Harrison, *The Early Victorians* (Weidenfeld & Nicolson, 1971)

16 G. Best, *Mid Victorian Britain* (Weidenfeld & Nicolson, 1971)

17 J. Foster, *Class Struggle and the Industrial Revolution. Early industrial capitalism in three English towns* (Weidenfeld & Nicolson, 1974)

18 H. J. Dyos and M. Wolff, *The Victorian City*, 2 vols (Routledge & Kegan Paul, 1973)

19 A. Briggs, 'The language of "class" in early nineteenth-century England', in A. Briggs and J. Saville, *Essays in Labour History* (Macmillan, 1960), also reprinted in M. W. Flinn and T. C. Smout, *Essays in Social History* (Oxford University Press, 1974)

20 A. Briggs, *Victorian Cities* (1963) (Penguin, 1968)

POLITICAL ORIGINS AND OTHER MOVEMENTS

21 D. Read, *The English Provinces* (Arnold, 1964)

21a D. Read, *Press and People, 1790–1850: opinion in three English cities* (Arnold, 1961) – on Leeds, Manchester and Sheffield

22 E. P. Thompson, *The Making of the English Working Class* (1963) (Penguin, 1968)

23 E. Royle, *Radical Politics 1790–1900; religion and unbelief* (Longman, 1971)

23a E. Royle and J. Walvin, *English Radicals and Reformers, 1760–1848* (Harvester, 1982)

23b J. R. Dinwiddy, *From Luddism to Chartism* (Historical Association, 1986)

23c M. Thomis and P. Holt, *Threats of Revolution in Britain, 1789–1848* (Macmillan, 1977)

24 D. G. Wright, *Democracy and Reform, 1815–1885* (Longman, 1970)

25 G. B. M. Finlayson, *England in the Eighteen-thirties: decade of reform* (Arnold, 1969)

26 J. T. Ward, ed., *Popular Movements 1830–1850* (Macmillan, 1970)

27 J. F. C. Harrison, *Robert Owen and the Owenites in Britain and America* (Routledge, 1968)

28 J. Wiener, *The War of the Unstamped* (Cornell University Press, 1969)

29 P. Hollis, *Pauper Press* (Oxford University Press, 1970)

30 J. T. Ward, *The Factory Movement* (Macmillan, 1962)

31 N. C. Edsall, *The Anti Poor Law Movement 1834–1844* (Manchester University Press, 1971)

31a J. Knott, *Popular Opposition to the 1834 Poor Law* (Croom Helm, 1986)

32 E. Royle, *Victorian Infidels* (Manchester University Press, 1974)

33 N. McCord, *The Anti-Corn-Law League.* (Unwin, 1958)

34 D. Read, *Cobden and Bright: a Victorian political partnership* (Arnold, 1967)

35 S. Webb and B. Webb, *The History of Trade Unionism* (Longman, 1920)

GENERAL STUDIES OF CHARTISM

36 M. Hovell, *The Chartist Movement* (Manchester University Press, 1918)

37 J. T. Ward, *Chartism* (Macmillan, 1973)

38 D. Jones, *Chartism and the Chartists* (Allen Lane, 1975)

38a D. Thompson, *The Chartists* (Temple Smith, 1984)

39 F. C. Mather, *Chartism*, Historical Association pamphlet G.61 (1965)

40 A. Wilson, 'Chartism', in J. T. Ward (**26**)

AUTOBIOGRAPHIES AND BIOGRAPHIES

41 S. Bamford, *Passages in the Life of a Radical* (T. Fisher Unwin, 1893)

42 W. Lovett, *Life and Struggles of William Lovett* (Trübner, 1876)

43 T. Cooper, *The Life of Thomas Cooper* (1872), new edition with an introduction by J. Saville (Leicester University Press, 1971)

44 T. Frost, *Forty Years' Recollections* (Sampson Low, &c., 1880)

45 W. E. Adams, *Memoirs of a Social Atom* (1903), new edition with an introduction by J. Saville (Kelley, 1968)

46 C. Shaw, *When I was a Child* (1903), new edition (Caliban Books, 1977)

47 D. Vincent, ed., *Testaments of Radicalism: memoirs of working-class politicians 1790–1885* (Europa, 1977); includes (a) *The Reminiscences of James Watson* (1854), (b) *The Reminiscences of Thomas Dunning* (1894), (c) J. J. Bezer, *The Autobiography of one of the Chartist Rebels of 1848* (1851), (d) B. Wilson, *The Struggles of an Old Chartist* (1887)

48 G. D. H. Cole, *Chartist Portraits* (1941) (Macmillan, 1965), contains chapters on Lovett, Stephens, Oastler, Attwood, Frost, Sturge, Cooper, Fielden, O'Brien, Harney, O'Connor, and Jones.

49 G. Wallas, *The Life of Francis Place* (Longman, 1898)

49a J. Belchem, *'Orator' Hunt. Henry Hunt and English Working Class Radicalism* (Clarendon Press, 1985)

50 A. G. Barker, *Henry Hetherington 1792–1849* (Pioneer Press, 1938)

51 C. Driver, *Tory Radical: the life of Richard Oastler* (1946) (Octagon, 1970)

52 D. Williams, *John Frost: a study in Chartism* (1939) (Evelyn, Adams & Mackay, 1969)

53 A. R. Schoyen, *The Chartist Challenge: a portrait of George Julian Harney* (Heinemann, 1958)

54 D. Read and E. Glasgow, *Feargus O'Connor. Irishman and Chartist* (Arnold, 1961)

54a J. Epstein, *The Lion of Freedom: Feargus O'Connor and the Chartist Movement, 1832–1842* (Croom Helm, 1982)

55 A. Plummer, *Bronterre: a political biography of Bronterre O'Brien 1804–1864* (Allen & Unwin, 1971)

56 J. Saville, *Ernest Jones: Chartist* (Lawrence & Wishart, 1952), includes a selection of Jones's writings

57 D. Large, 'William Lovett', in P. Hollis, ed., *Pressure from Without in Early Victorian England* (Arnold, 1974)

58 B. Harrison, 'Henry Vincent', in *Dictionary of Labour Biography* vol. I (Macmillan, 1972)

59 B. Harrison and P. Hollis, 'Chartism, Liberalism and Robert Lowery', *English Historical Review* lxxxii (1967)

59a B. Harrison and P. Hollis, *Robert Lowery: Radical and Chartist* (Europa, 1979) – edited autobiography

60 S. Chadwick, *'A Bold and Faithful Journalist', Joshua Hobson 1810–1876* (Kirklees Metropolitan Council, 1976)

61 J. T. Ward, 'Centenary of Lawrence Pitkeithley's death', *Huddersfield Daily Examiner*, 2 June, 1958

61a J. T. Ward, 'Revolutionary Tory: the life of J. R. Stephens', *Transactions of the Lancashire and Cheshire Antiquarian Society* xvii (1958)

LOCAL STUDIES

62 A. Briggs, ed., *Chartist Studies* (Macmillan 1959); includes (a) D. Read, 'Chartism in Manchester', (b) J. F. C.

Harrison, 'Chartism in Leeds', (c) J. F. C. Harrison, 'Chartism in Leicester', (d) H. Fearn, 'Chartism in Suffolk', (e) R. B. Pugh, 'Chartism in Somerset and Wiltshire', (f) D. Williams, 'Chartism in Wales', (g) A. Wilson, Chartism in Glasgow'.

63 J. Epstein and D. Thompson, eds, *The Chartist Experience* (Macmillan, 1982); includes (a) C. Behagg on the Birmingham Political Union, (b) J. Bennett on the London Democratic Association, (c) D. Thompson on Ireland and the Irish, (d) R. Sykes on Early Chartism and Trade Unionism in South-East Lancashire, (e) R. Fyson on the Potteries in 1842, (f) J. Epstein on Nottingham, (g) K. Tiller on late Chartism in Halifax.

64 D. J. Rowe, 'The Chartist Convention and the Regions', *Economic History Review* xxii (1969)

65 D. Goodway, *London Chartism, 1838–1848* (Cambridge University Press, 1982)

65a D. J. Rowe, 'The failure of London Chartism', *Historical Journal* xi, no. 3 (1968)

65b D. J. Rowe, 'Chartism and the Spitalfields Weavers', *Economic History Review* xx (1967)

65c I. J. Prothero, 'Chartism in London', *Past & Present* no. 44 (August 1967)

65d I. J. Prothero, 'London Chartism and the Trades', *Economic History Review* xxiv (1971)

65e I. J. Prothero, *Artisans and Politics in Early Nineteenth Century London* (Methuen, 1981)

65f D. Large 'London in the Year of Revolutions, 1848', in J. Stevenson, ed., *London in the Age of Reform* (Blackwell, 1977)

66 J. Cannon, *The Chartists in Bristol*, Bristol Branch of the Historical Association, Local History Pamphlet no. 10 (1964)

67 A. F. J. Brown, *Chartism in Essex and Suffolk* (Essex Record Office & Suffolk Libraries and Archives, 1982)

68 D. J. Rowe, 'Tyneside Chartism', in N. McCord, ed., *Essays in Tyneside Labour History* (Newcastle upon Tyne Polytechnic, 1977)

69 A. J. Peacock, *Bradford Chartism 1838–1840*, University of York, Borthwick Papers no. 36 (1969)

69a J. Salt, *Chartism in South Yorkshire*, University of Sheffield Institute of Education, Local History Pamphlets no. 1 (1967)

69b J. L. Baxter, 'Early Chartism and Labour Class Struggle:

South Yorkshire, 1837–40', in S. Pollard and C. Holmes, eds, *Essays in the Economic and Social History of South Yorkshire* (South Yorkshire County Council, 1976)

70 P. Searby, *Coventry Politics in the Age of the Chartists*, Coventry Branch of the Historical Association (1964)

70a P. Searby, 'Chartists and Freemen in Coventry', *Social History* no. 6 (October 1977)

71 T. Tholfsen, 'The Chartist crisis in Birmingham', *International Review of Social History* iii, no. 3 (1958)

71a C. Flick, *The Birmingham Political Union and the reform movements in Britain, 1830–1839* (Dawson, 1978)

72 L. C. Wright, *Scottish Chartism* (Oliver & Boyd, 1953)

72a A. Wilson, *The Chartist Movement in Scotland* (Manchester University Press, 1970)

73 D. J. V. Jones, *The Last Rising. The Newport Insurrection of 1839* (Oxford University Press, 1985)

73a I. Wilks, *South Wales and the Rising of 1839* (Croom Helm, 1984)

74 R. O'Higgins, 'The Irish influence on the Chartist Movement', *Past and Present* no. 20 (1961)

74a J. H. Treble, 'O'Connor, O'Connell and the attitudes of Irish Immigrants towards Chartism in the North of England, 1838–48', in J. Butt and I. F. Clarke, eds, *The Victorians and Social Protest* (David & Charles, 1973)

SPECIAL ASPECTS OF CHARTISM

75 G. Kitson Clark, 'Hunger and politics in 1842', *Journal of Modern History* xxv, no. 4 (1953)

76 A. Jenkin, 'Chartism and the trade unions', in L. M. Munby, *The Luddites and other essays* (Katanka, 1971)

77 A. G. Rose, 'The Plug Riots of 1842 in Lancashire and Cheshire', *Transactions of the Lancashire and Cheshire Antiquarian Society* lxvii (1957)

78 F. C. Mather, 'The General Strike of 1842', in J. Stevenson and R. Quinault, eds, *Popular Protest and Public Order* (Allen & Unwin, 1974)

78a M. Jenkins, *The General Strike of 1842* (Lawrence & Wishart, 1980)

78b J. Stevenson, *Popular Disturbances in England, 1700–1870* (Longman, 1979)

79 B. Simon, *Studies in the History of Education 1780–1870* (1960), reissued as *The Two Nations and the Educational Structure 1780–1870* (Lawrence & Wishart, 1974); see chapter 5 for Chartist educational activities.

80 H. U. Faulkener, *Chartism and the Churches* (1916) (Cass, 1970)

80a E. Yeo, 'Christianity in Chartist Struggle', *Past & Present* no. 91 (May 1981)

81 R. F. Wearmouth, *Some Working-Class Movements of the Nineteenth Century* (Epworth, 1948) – see section 2, chapters ii–v for Chartism, with emphasis on Methodist influences.

82 T. Tholfsen, *Working-Class Radicalism in mid-Victorian England* (Croom Helm, 1976); see chapter 3 for Chartist culture.

82a G. Stedman Jones, 'The Language of Chartism', in Epstein and Thompson (**63**)

83 E. Yeo, 'Robert Owen and radical culture', in S. Pollard and J. Salt, eds, *Robert Owen, Prophet of the Poor* (Macmillan, 1971); contains much also on Chartist culture.

83a E. Yeo, 'Culture and Constraint in Working-class Movements, 1830–1855', in E. & S. Yeo, eds, *Popular Culture and Class Conflict, 1590–1914* (Harvester, 1981)

83b E. Yeo, 'Some Practices and Problems of Chartist Democracy', in Epstein & Thompson (**63**)

84 J. Simon (translated), 'Chartist literature' – introduction to Y.V. Kovalev (**11**), in L. M. Munby, ed., *The Luddites* (Katanka, 1971)

85 F. F. Rosenblatt, *The Chartist Movement in its Social and Economic Aspects* (1916) (Cass, 1970)

86 F. C. Mather, *Public Order in the Age of the Chartists* (Manchester University Press, 1959)

86a F. C. Mather, 'The Government and the Chartists', in A. Briggs, ed., *Chartist Studies* (**62**)

86b C. Godfrey, 'The Chartist Prisoners, 1839–1841', *International Review of Social History* xxiv (1979)

87 D. Thompson, 'Women and Nineteenth-century Radical Politics: a lost dimension', in J. Mitchell and A. Oakley, eds, *The Rights and Wrongs of Women* (Penguin, 1976)

87a D. Jones, 'Women and Chartism', *History* vol. 68 (1983)

87b M. Thomis and J. Grimmett, *Women in Protest* (Croom Helm, 1982)

88 D. J. Rowe, 'The London Working Men's Association and the "People's Charter"', *Past and Present* no. 36 (April 1967), and the subsequent debate with I. Prothero in *Past and Present* no. 38 (December 1968)

88a J. Belchem, 'Chartism and the Trades', *English Historical Review* lxcviii (1983)

89 J. Belchem, '1848: Feargus O'Connor and the Collapse of the Mass Platform', in Epstein and Thompson (**63**)

89a H. Weisser, *April 10. Challenge and Response in England in 1848* (University Press of America, 1983)

90 H. Weisser, *British Working Class Movements and Europe 1815–1848* (Manchester University Press, 1975)

90a H. Weisser, 'Chartist Internationalism', *Historical Journal* xiv, no. 1 (1971)

90b E. Kamenka and F. B. Smith, eds., *Intellectuals and Revolution: socialism and the experience of 1848* (Arnold, 1979)

91 R. Shannon, 'David Urquhart and the Foreign Affairs Committees', in P. Hollis, ed., *Pressure from Without* (Arnold, 1974)

92 A. M. Hadfield, *The Chartist Land Company* (David & Charles, 1970)

93 J. MacAskill, 'The Chartist Land Plan', in A. Briggs, *Chartist Studies* (**62**)

94 L. Brown, 'The Chartists and the Anti-Corn Law League', in A. Briggs, *Chartist Studies* (**62**)

95 B. Harrison, 'Teetotal Chartism', *History*, no. 193 (June 1973)

96 J. A. Epstein, 'Feargus O'Connor and the *Northern Star*', *International Review of Social History* xxi (1976)

LATTERDAY CHARTISM

97 P. W. Slosson, *The Decline of the Chartist Movement* (1916) (Cass, 1967)

97a D. Thompson, 'Chartism, Success or Failure?', in D. Rubinstein, ed., *People for the People. Radical Ideas and Personalities in British History* (Ithaca Press, 1973)

97b J. Saville, 'Chartism in the Year of Revolution', *Modern Quarterly* viii (1952)

98 F. E. Gillespie, *Labour and Politics in England 1850–1867* (1927) (Cass, 1966)

99 S. Shipley, *Club Life and Socialism in Mid Victorian London*, History Workshop Pamphlet no. 5. Ruskin College, Oxford (1971)

100 G. Barnsby, 'Chartism in the Black Country 1850–1860', in L. M. Munby, *The Luddites* (Katanka, 1971)

NOVELS ABOUT CHARTISTS
101 B. Disraeli, *Sybil, or the Two Nations* (1845)
102 E. Gaskell, *Mary Barton* (1847)
103 C. Kingsley, *Alton Locke* (1850)
104 G. Eliot, *Felix Holt, the Radical* (1866)

ADDITIONAL REFERENCES
105 L. Faucher, *Manchester in 1844* (1844) (Cass, 1969)
106 *Cause of the People*, 20 May, 1848
107 G. Kitson Clark, 'The Romantic element', in J. H. Plumb, ed., *Studies in Social History* (Longman, 1955)
108 G. J. Holyoake, *Sixty Years of an Agitator's Life* (T. Fisher Unwin, 1892)
109 *Republican*, 1 June, 1871
110 Prince Albert to Lord John Russell, 10 April, 1848 (*Letters of Queen Victoria*)
111 B. Brierley, *Failsworth, My Native Village* (Oldham, 1895)
112 *National Reformer*, 20, 27 July, 1861
113 R. Harrison, 'The 10th April of Spencer Walpole', *International Review of Social History* vii (1962)
114 *Newcastle Daily Chronicle*, 24 September, 1877

Index